# What readers are saying:

*The book is an amazing read. It pulls you in with a fascinating story of the author's experience, of the experiences of her clients as well as a framework of guiding principles to live a deeper truer experience of your life. There is the neuroscience also to support the orientation and wisdom held in this book. If you read the book you will get more than you can imagine. The value and teachings in this book are amazing and fully life serving.*

*Thanks for putting out this wonderful book that is sure to influence and bring a whole realm of new possibilities to others.*

Primitivo Rojas, MD

*Thanks so much for your book. What amazing insights! As expected, this is a wonderful, flowing, congruent writing by an expert in the field of inner wisdom and life satisfaction. I want to highlight how important I think this book is.*

*"Staying in the Light: How To Integrate the Nine Wisdoms From Your Soul" is a concrete self-help book about the journey of spirit. Morrin Bass is an expert in spirituality, leadership and guidance derived through deeply developed methodology of higher consciousness work. The book takes us on her journey into the wisdom of the spirit expressed from the inner world of each client.*

*The nine wisdoms are profound messages of the soul and of the spirit, that speak to our higher self expression, that need to be heard by everyone. Peppered with her own experiences from mystical motherland to Wall Street and then into the world of the inner truth, Morrin examines the practical steps how to tap into "the magic that comes from inside all of us," in creating personal satisfaction and life success.*

*There are wisdoms how we can become our authentic selves and help others become aware, how to "focus on what you love to do," as an occupation in life, how to create "balance in your body" and soul for better health and happier lives. Morrin uses the metaphor of spiritual guidance to teach how to "allow the mind to follow the structure of peace, love and balance, purity and presence," and how to choose love, compassion and peace as our daily bread.*

*I had the great fortune to film a session with Morrin breathtakingly connecting with her light adept at showing people "what to do with the light" when it comes to their own lives. She's truly an evolved being, and her book should be part of any person's library who is seeking to find out the truth about why we are on the planet and what we're meant to do with our time here.*

*Highly recommended!*

Rich Martini, author *Flipside: A Tourist's Guide on How to Navigate the Afterlife.*

Morrin's book "Staying In The Light" is a deep analysis of the wisdoms from the soul told in an easy to read style with science references and clients stories. I love Morrin's incredible personal story, making sense of the wisdom count bringing to front the utilization of helpful ways we forget or avoid. Highly recommend this book for all those who seek the truth and inner connection. Thanks for the enlightening read!

Cecilia Beltran, author, *Darkness Before Light*

"Staying In The Light" is a philosophy of a new kind of leadership, the one that includes our soul, a spiritual awareness leadership. In a workplace, where corporate rules are strong, people long for spirituality and acknowledgement of their inner world and personal value. Besides, connection with inner wisdom and awareness helps them be more attentive, more conscious, and do their job with more depth and dedication. "Staying In The Light" is particularly valuable in my area of educating the medical staff and emergency technicians, because that way they are more attentive to their patients and the patients' satisfaction improves, as we help humanity stay healthy. Thank you for putting these ideas out for the corporate world.

Karla Solorzano, CH,
Professional Educator for Medical and Nursing Staff,
Maimonides Hospital, New York

# STAYING IN THE LIGHT:

# HOW TO INTEGRATE THE 9 WISDOMS FROM YOUR SOUL

A Manifesto
for successful people who are looking to
succeed further, with
deeper meaning and satisfaction

by Morrin Bass, PhD

**BALBOA**
PRESS
A DIVISION OF HAY HOUSE

Balboa Press books may be ordered through booksellers or by contacting:

Balboa Press
A Division of Hay House
1663 Liberty Drive
Bloomington, IN 47403
www.balboapress.com
1-(877) 407-4847

Because of the dynamic nature of the Internet, any web addresses or links contained in
this book may have changed since publication and may no longer be valid. The views
expressed in this work are solely those of the author and do not necessarily reflect the
views of the publisher, and the publisher hereby disclaims any responsibility for them.

The author of this book does not dispense medical advice or prescribe the use of any
technique as a form of treatment for physical, emotional, or medical problems without the
advice of a physician, either directly or indirectly. The intent of the author is only to offer
information of a general nature to help you in your quest for emotional and spiritual well-
being. In the event you use any of the information in this book for yourself, which is your
constitutional right, the author and the publisher assume no responsibility for your actions.

Front Cover art – Emergence, oil on canvas, original
artwork by Morrin Bass, Copyright(C) 2003

Back Cover art - Transformation, oil on canvas, original
artwork by Morrin Bass, Copyright(C) 2003

Morrin's own transpersonal experiences are expressed in her own painting, a hobby
she enjoys. As a professional artist, Morrin is often inspired to an experience by her
clients' transpersonal experiences and visions, and reflects her client's revelations in her
paintings. Exclusive private clients enjoy those on special commissions. The painting
then becomes for them an anchor and a reminder of their experience, and a frequent
point of connection, a portal to their own wisdom, guidance and enlightenment.

To order additional copies of this book please contact New York Awareness Center at
NewYorkAwarenessCenter@gmail.com. Find more information at
www.NewYorkAwarenessCenter.com and www.MorrinBass.com

Printed in the United States of America
ISBN: 978-1-4525-6794-5 (sc)
ISBN: 978-1-4525-6795-2 (e)

Balboa Press rev. date: 02/21/2013

*To my partner Mark*

*The essence of all beautiful art, all great art, is gratitude.*
Friedrich Nietzsche

# Foreword

*What is essential in a work of art is that
it should rise above the realm of personal and
speak to the spirit and heart of the poet as
man to the spirit and heart of mankind.*

—Carl Gustav Jung

Life is a work of art. Creating this work of art one must express themselves fully with all their potential. This is the essence of life: living the life, and living it to the fullest. And then comes a time when they want to give to others, and they have to say it, write it, dance it, paint it, for others to see the amazing world of wonder they possess, so that others too may turn inside to see their own world, and their own true potential, opportunity and desire, so they too can enhance their life and the life of others with the richness of the wisdom from their soul.

*Staying In The Light* is a beautiful book expressing a clear and concise view on how to become fulfilled, and a way to show the reader that what they are longing for is just a step away; a journey to soul, and an analysis of wisdoms on the path already walked by the author.

Morrin's work reflects her passion and personality, being a creative director of her world. She models a life inside success she created for herself. It is noted how readily others respond to her charming and gracious being. As she begins her work, in groups or in person, the results are achieved quickly and efficiently.

The book inspires interest in the work that Morrin does. She is a passionate individual and a thorough professional. Morrin is a provocative yet gentle catalyst for deep transformational experience of your soul's wisdom and practical steps to your further success.

Dr. Bass naturally blends her intuitive spirituality and strong leadership, scientifically supporting her unconventional ways of creating new angle of utilizing spiritual awareness in the work place and at home. Her inspiring presentations and workshops for women-entrepreneurs, and speaking to groups in a corporate environment and associations helped create her a reputation of a mythical being, powerful spirit, and a charming representative of a new generation of spiritual leaders who gets you to the place of the results you desire.

*Staying In The Light* is a hand-book reflecting Morrin's views on the way of decision making through a state of heightened awareness and from a position of balance and wisdom, challenging one's beliefs, provoking thoughts and awareness. Morrin's idea is to inspire you toward living a fulfilled and purposeful life of satisfaction coupled with personal success and happiness.

*I don't have to have faith, I have experience.*

—Joseph Campbell

# Contents

# Preface

## Discover Your Direct Line to the Divine

*We are not human beings having a spiritual experience.*
*We are spiritual beings having a human experience.*

—Teilhard de Chardin

Assembling the wisdoms of the soul work into a book *Staying in the Light* appeared as an idea after my return from a working trip to Israel in February 2012. I had enough material working in this direction for the last 10 years, yet the transformational nature of my work with a group in Israel started the ball rolling. I had been invited by a woman seeking an experienced specialist to facilitate her transpersonal self-discovery in the critical period in her life.

In September 2011, after finishing my work for the day, I had looked through some social media messages and found this woman's question. She wanted to have a personal experience facilitated by a specialist connecting with her inner truth, inner guidance helping define clarity, yet she couldn't find a local specialist in Israel. We agreed that I would travel to work with her in person. I knew how to make my trip economically feasible because I had successfully done it two years earlier.

In 2009, a different woman from Israel had written directly to me, similarly out of the blue, searching for a transpersonal specialist to redefine her life's meaning after a tragic loss of her twin sister in a car crash. I felt I had to help. My partner, Mark, and I traveled to Israel 3 months later to work with an interested group of people she had managed to assemble. Each of them were searching for their life's meaning through transpersonal connection, that I facilitated.

This time, after I finished the personal work, I spoke to the group of my discoveries, highlighting the aspects of individual experiences and reflecting on the patterns that came up for most participants. Bringing in the years of work in this specialty which allowed me to see clearly the astonishing similarity of the revealed wisdom for each participant, I spoke of the truths that came up for them. There, across the world from my home in New York, I stood in front of the group of seekers whose backgrounds were as diverse as many of my journeyers back home. They were university professors, corporate executives, artists, entertainers, spiritual leaders, actors, technical directors, inventors, business owners, and housewives. The truths revealed to them through their wisdom guidance were consistent with what I had been recording elsewhere.

*Staying in the Light: How to Integrate the Nine Truths of Wisdom From Your Soul*, became this book, defining an idea of living on purpose and providing easy and concise reference for successful people who are on the path of spiritual self-discovery and who want more success in other areas in their lives and desire the ability to make higher-quality decisions for life and work.

Having come from a corporate background, I know how much quality decision-making strategies are needed and appreciated among the executives of the world. I wanted to write a reference book to reflect the idea of mindful effectiveness in the workplace and in personal lives. Based on the principles of my work, my ethics, and my aesthetic of life emerging from the concept of "being in the light," I bring my experience and passion for work with others toward the experience of themselves in the light in creating their life with intention and meaning.

Before writing this book, I decided to organize the material I had collected over the years in one concise white-paper presentation reflecting my views and methodology in order to facilitate organization of my speaking engagements for corporate workshops and keynote speeches at conferences and organizational meetings. This time my deadline became the annual National Guild of Hypnotists (NGH) Convention in August, a gathering of professionals at which I am a key-note presenter as faculty member. My presentation was titled "Success Is a Journey With The Light."

# Introduction

## What Is "Staying in the Light"?

*It is better to light a candle than curse the darkness.*

—Eleanor Roosevelt

Many people come to me with questions, looking for meaning in their lives. It's not that they have no idea what their life is about, it's just they don't know how to begin to place value on the years of achieving and creating. Often in our forties and fifties, or even in our thirties, we begin to seek confirmation of what has been happening in our lives so far in a spiritual sense of soul-searching and life purpose. It is at this time in life that many turn to "God," a higher power that controls them from the outside, only to find that the control is up to them, that the meaning of life is what meaning they attach to it, and with what perspective they look at their own story.

"Staying in the light" is a facilitated process that connects individuals to their personal wisdom and inner guidance, to their own truth. "Staying in the light" is unique, as it helps a person uncover his or her personal life's intention from the position of balance. It is easy to commit to a decision made form a position of balance, and therefore, the inner connection is powerful; the true life direction uncovered from balance creates transformational long lasting change. The incredible power of following self-discovery in the state of meditative awareness, facilitated by clarity of choice and immanency of commitment, creates for the individual a strong link to legacy and satisfaction from the process, leading to finding satisfaction in aspects of their life that are most fulfilling and meaningful. My clients enjoy highly personalized creative processes of their own connections to their inner truth and personal wisdom.

The work I do is accompanied by a sense of well-being, an inner knowing of what to do next, and the discovery of the meaning of one's life. "Staying in the light" reflects the individual's personal mythology, which reveals his or her internal organization, beliefs, and values and simplifies decision making.

Connection with the divine uncovering an individual's intentions is also a pivotal point of change so that the desired transformation in the appropriate direction can take place. By observing a client's internal mythology, I connect the physiology of the body in its balanced form with the neuroscience and lead the client to his or her place of wisdom, where emerges the sense of a bigger picture, an awareness of life direction, a legacy, and a long-desired sense of personal satisfaction. I facilitate clients' experiences of their own wisdom in their own terms, create space where doubt dissipates, and create awareness through a unique series of intention-based protocols in higher consciousness, leading them to create a desired future that is in line with who they are. As a mentor, I help clients further connect to the information in connection with their intentions. Together we uncover ways to make active decisions for everyday living using their patterns of success.

# Is This Right for You?

*A mind that is stretched by a new experience*
*can never go back to its old dimensions.*
—Oliver Wendell Holmes, Jr.

I often hear about dreams people have in which they experience their lives somehow differently—better, richer, fuller, in more complete and satisfying ways, with a sense of adventure and the unknown, where life begins to make sense. Others seek a higher consciousness experience of connecting with their spirituality, guidance, and power as an effective way to create impactful solutions for situations that are unavailable to the conscious mind alone. Still others want scientifically proven and traditional yet cutting-edge ways of mind mapping for creating future memories of their lives' intentions.

If you find yourself relating to one of the categories above, as a seeker of a fuller, richer, more meaningful life, with satisfaction, this book is for you.

Read this book now if at some point in your life you have already experienced success, tasted various experiences, been touched by disappointments from other people's expectations of you, and now find yourself asking the following fundamental questions:

- What have I accomplished?

- How can I make my life even better and sustain it?

- What is the meaning of my life?

In early 2001, through a series of auspicious circumstances that I describe later in the book, I came upon the realization of the power of the mind. When I began to search for a deeper meaning of my own life,

I experimented with the power of *my* mind and found that self-suggestion, dreams, meditative states, artistic creation, and spirituality are all related. I discovered that the secret of *my* potential was inside *me*, and I wanted to find ways to realize it quickly and effectively. I embarked on a journey. I found a treasure, studied it, researched it, made sure it worked, and went on to share it with others.

Reflecting on the decade of my work with clients, I have felt guided to the conclusions I lay out in this book: that we are all loved, that we all have a purpose, and that we all need to stay in the light and fulfill ourselves. Simple daily practice of staying in balance, congruency, and integrity with yourself and your inner wisdom—essentially, staying in the light—recommended by spiritual guides bring great benefits both in the short term and in the long term and are easy to implement.

In my work providing clients with a bridge to spiritual freedom, satisfaction, and awareness, I have collected stories, questions, and topics that reflect their experiences. I have punctuated those experiences with notes of what was relevant for them in their experiences, as well as reflections from my own journey. I am here to reveal to you one more angle of how your life's journey can be breathtaking.

Read this book with an open heart as part of your path to discovering your own legacy in the time when you allow your guidance, trusted advice, and solid ground to guide you to your truth.

## Be Yourself

*People are capable, at any time in their lives, of doing what they dream of.*

—Paulo Coelho, *The Alchemist*

When I began experimenting with alternative modalities,

I experienced a revelation. An angel holding a book appeared to me. A column of light penetrated the title page. I thumbed through the book, but its pages were empty. I was given a task to write in those pages. The next ten years became a journey to fill them.

I couldn't write the book I wanted being who I was then. I had to first rediscover who I am.

For years I heard the expression, "Be yourself." I didn't know what that meant. I was dissatisfied. Something was missing. I often found myself confused. I put myself in situations that made me even more confused. I spent years searching for explanations of who I was so that I could feel whole, complete, and satisfied.

Then I came upon a way to know who I am. It was like being reborn, recognizing myself inside the debris of accumulated beliefs and someone else's values that I could peel off. Many call it finding peace, inner truth, wisdom, satisfaction; attaining *satori*; or letting go. I could begin to enjoy being myself, loving myself, allowing my true being shine through. I was finally able to put my attention on what was important, make high-quality decisions, and generate a highly functional, balanced life.

The book embracing the concept of *Staying in the Light* emerged as a result of that journey, reflecting my genuine passion and curiosity for the human mind, inner wisdom, brain science, and revisiting self-awareness and balance.

Spiritual guides often actively withhold bits of information as part of the wisdom to leave you to begin to explore and create on your own as you interpret the meaning of their guidance. I am here to offer you a provocative perspective on how the extraordinary wisdom can enrich your life.

So let's begin again.

# Nine Truths of Wisdom

*The black moment is the moment when*
*the real message of transformation is going to come.*
*At the darkest moment comes the light.*

—Joseph Campbell

Wisdom experienced from higher consciousness carries wise and loving instructions. In this book, I identify nine truths of wisdom. Regardless of the structure of the session and the clients' beliefs, these are the major directions to which spiritual guidance consistently points. So these Wisdoms are as follows:

I.    Life is a story. You are the writer and the hero in your own story, and your story is malleable. It is just a story based on previous beliefs, and you can change the narrative if you want.

II.    Be in balance. Find your balance and stay in balance; without balance there is no flow.

III.    Relax. Understand the importance of relaxation and use deep rejuvenating breaths to restore and sustain balance through relaxation and rejuvenation.

IV.    Do what you love. Do the best you can to live your life willingly and lovingly, and simultaneously, actively, do not do what you don't love.

V.    Have fun. It is important to have fun, to stop being so serious about everything, and to stop worrying. Enjoy life all the way.

VI.    Exercise. Exercising your physical body and your brain is of utmost importance.

VII.    Stay in the light. Keep a positive attitude, gratitude, and love as main core values, add the "light" to all activities, and make it a common thread for your life experience.

VIII. Live with intention. Having a mindful approach is vital if you want to achieve anything. It is hard to get someplace if you don't know where you are headed. Maintain clarity on what you want and how to take the next step toward it. Always keep the long-term outcome in mind.

IX. Contemplate your contribution to the world. Do the right thing. Find your place in the universal plan. Find meaning to your actions. Establish a direction to begin creating your own legacy and contribution to the world. Decide that you must follow this plan.

I continue to find that individual variations of personal discoveries largely fall into the nine categories above, almost to the word expressed to each individual.

## Guides

*Just as treasures are uncovered from the earth, so*
*virtue appears from good deeds, and*
*wisdom appears from a pure and peaceful mind.*
*To walk safely through the maze of human life, one needs*
*the light of wisdom and the guidance of virtue.*

−Buddha

Often a question comes up: Who is guiding me? Who answers my questions? What are they, our guides? Are they real? How does one become aware of this guidance and trust them? How do we stay connected to their wisdom?

Once we are in a realm of higher awareness, transformation of consciousness and connection happens. Spiritual guides appear and offer their wisdom in response to questions asked or help requested. Depending on a person's background, religious beliefs, and personal history, one can experience guides as any number of advisors, from angels to ancestors, totem animals to wispy spirits, or even just as a sensation of a wise presence—in a visual format or not. Spiritual guidance is often available in a symbolic form corresponding to our belief system, and comes as an angel, or an ancestor. Transpersonal awareness is always filled with the abundance of wisdom, and positive attitude. In the realm of higher consciousness guides always offer wisdom with humor, love, and support that show in the answers to our questions and make my work very enjoyable and rewarding.

Serious inquiries such as "Why am I here?" "Who am I?" and "What am I supposed to do with my life?" are answered with easy-going and candid wisdom. To discover these answers simplifies the overall complexity of human existence. The feature I like the most is the useful, direct, and to-the-point wisdom from spiritual guides that represent our own inner wisdom and the wise inner voice with a definite positive bias. Permissive and caring, this wise inner voice clearly shows us that we are in charge of our lives and that no one else can assume the responsibility for our lives and actions. Once we know what to do, it is up to us to do it or not do it.

That is the real choice.

# Wisdom I: Life Is a Story

## A Story as Just a Story

*Let your mind start a journey thru a strange new world.*
*Leave all thoughts of the world you knew before.*
*Let your soul take you where you long to be …*
*Close your eyes let your spirit start to soar, and*
*you'll live as you've never lived before.*

—Erich Fromm

## Life Is a Story

*You are what you believe yourself to be.*
—Paulo Coelho, *The Witch of Portobello*

We all live inside stories. These stories are the narratives we offer about ourselves, and they contain organizing principles of who we believe ourselves to be.

We live our lives according to those principles.

What's interesting is that those organizing principles are operating through us, yet most often they remain outside of our awareness.

When asked, "Who are you?" I used to say, "I am my parent's daughter" or "I am an executive" or "I am an American." I believed I *was* my role. The idea of identity totally escaped me.

Most of us act according to a system of beliefs, values, symbols, and criteria of which we are not even aware. It is difficult to look at our situations from another point of view. It is not our fault.Our beliefs and values become our identities.

Look at it from another standpoint. When you were born, there were no values, no beliefs, and no roles. Yet you were still you. What makes you - you?

What is the story you are telling the world about yourself? How does it serve you? How does it serve others around you? What would you like to change in that story? And what would you leave the same?

Who are you? What is your story?

## What's in a Story?

*We must be willing to let go of the life we planned so as to have the life that is waiting for us.*

—Joseph Campbell

In the wisdom state, the story that underlays the informative flow is consistent with the story of your cultural background, present beliefs, and values accumulated over the years of upbringing, living in an environment, and being influenced by certain authorities in your life. Some people believe in past lives, reincarnation, spiritual enlightenment; others look for a scientific approach, logical explanations. Whatever way your story unfolds, trust the information and keep the position of openness.

I am told I have an unusual background, although I think it is very normal. I grew up in Moscow, Russia during the Iron Curtain times, lacking basic choices. Fear was my normal emotion. I was afraid to speak my mind, let alone knowing what mind I had! Growing up, like everyone else, I was brainwashed in one direction, of taming my initiative, creativity and passions. I moved to the United States like Alice into Wonderland, completely fascinated and unable to hold myself from it. But let me tell you the story.

Back then it was called the Soviet Union. Although religion was discouraged by the State, the people of Russia remained (and still remain) very mystical. Their actions often indicate a belief that forces outside of themselves control even the most mundane daily acts. For example, Russians believe returning home for forgotten things is a bad omen. It is better to leave whatever you forgot behind, but if returning is necessary, one should look in the mirror before leaving the house again; otherwise, the journey will be unlucky.

I was not baptized into a religion until I was 24. Then I wanted to experiment with what the organized religion has to offer, as I was seeking an alternative to a political party activity. My parents were progressive atheists, not religious and only very lightly mystical mostly out of tradition. On my father's side my grandmother was very present to me, and I remember her wise teachings about puberty and marriage. She regularly and secretly for most of her life went to church and celebrated all orthodox holidays, despite the fact that she was married to a front line "bolshevik" - a general in the Red Army, who died in torture during Stalin times. Back then church and Red Army did not do well together, so I ate the Easter cakes at my granny's home without knowing what they meant and why we get to eat those treats only once a year. Much later in my life that I learned about the mythologies and rituals of Christianity, Theosophy, Buddhism, Judaism, Jainism, and I even went so far as to become an ordained minister. Fundamentally, I am not religious and don't belong to any church, but I consider myself a very spiritual person because spirituality means my own connection to the

3

absolute inside me. I view spirituality as self-quest to uncover a creative position inside and a connection to the world through self-alignment.

On my mother's side, I had no grandparents alive in my time, but my mom told me of her stern mother, married to a talented car engineer, an heir of a few beer factories in Moscow, who dreamt of moving to America to design cars for the Ford, which never came to life. Instead, my mom's father dies pursued for his creativity during the Stalin times as well.

My mother, a quiet, patient and educated lady, taught me to read at the age of four, and I grew to really like reading. I liked "good books," what we considered literature. Good books were scarce. In school we were given textbooks, and I often went to the library with a list of required reading, and read more than that list. My librarian took some books out from under her desk to help my fascination with folk tales, adventures and world literary gems. I was well versed in Soviet literature, but my awareness of literature from other countries was still limited.

As I grew up, government policies changed. Doors opened wider to the outside world, the Wonderland beyond the Iron Curtain. I could get my hands on books by foreign writers like John Updike, and I read *Run Rabbit Run*. I even read the previously forbidden Russians - Nabokov's *Lolita* and Pasternak's *Doctor Zhivago*. The only way I could get these books was to collect old newspapers and periodicals. Forty kilos of paper (85 pounds) would give me access to one book by a foreign writer. Now that was a good recycling policy. People no longer left newspapers on subway seats when they were done with them.

In my teenage years, I was hungry for knowledge. I loved to read and still do. I was happy if a friend lent me a book or if my parents brought home a book for a night. By the time I was fourteen or fifteen years old, my father, a well-known architect, became a director in a government architectural bureau. His mostly female employees occasionally sweetened his attitude with a forbidden or politically incorrect book, which he brought home. I remember reading whatever came to my hand at the time, sitting in my bed, propped up by pillows until 3:00 a.m. Unfortunately, much of the best literature was still banned; philosophy, psychology, and behavioral studies were considered controversial. Even Shakespeare was off the library shelves. The political party line was - the less people knew, the better off they were. I did not know who Mme Blavatsky was, but I could have plenty of Lenin.

Travel across borders was also forbidden. Visas to most places were unavailable. My first travel outside the Soviet Union was at age 24 to Prague, a part of the socialist friendly neighboring countries. There I drank beer for breakfast, lunch and dinner as part of the country's regimen, something I have never done up till then, enjoying it, and all the shiny objects around me. In Prague, I bought my first piece of clothing, a white skiing jacket; up till then, I sew my own clothes, because stores were poorly stocked.

On the other hand, my father, a prominent architect, was well recognized and was permitted to travel abroad frequently for work. I had a vivid experience of foreign places through his stories. When he returned from travel, we would sit in the kitchen, and I stared past his face into the scenes he described, open mouthed, as he told stories about amazing countries he visited, foreign people, and their extraordinary foods, clothes and behavior. Imagine, it was a dream world for me! When I was 11, my father traveled to New York to work with a team of American architects on the project of the Moscow World Trade Center, a complex that is now spread by the bank of the river Moskva. It was then when I learned about the fantastical country called America.

Again, there is a story connecting me with America.

Father kept secret for many years, that he had been offered to defect during the time of his work in New York, as many talented people were offered during the 1970s, and he refused! He couldn't leave my mom and me. We would have never seen him again, and would have probably been sent to Siberia, or some other restraining place. Who knows what would have happened to us if he had defected. Party line was strict.

My parents instilled in me strong values of family, personal integrity and good education. A postwar child, my mom taught me her best values—elegant styling, homemaking, piano playing, ballet, sewing, while my father taught me his—conceptual creativity, drawing, painting, and modeling, as well as achieving and succeeding. In retrospect, this was a combination of a perfect schooling for entertaining and business success! Yet, there was no intention for any specific direction in my life. Although I was taught skills and techniques, my parents did not teach me how to determine what I want in life, how to make decisions about what I wanted, and how to apply those skills to achieve what I wanted, because for the most part, there wasn't much to want. Choices were very limited, knowledge and exposure to other views weren't available.

Like many parents, mine simply wished me the best; they did not want me *not* to have what they had lacked. Both of them were educated as professional architects, and they truly believed that architectural school offered the most promise for the practical success they wanted for me. Back then I held my parents as authorities and followed their direction.

The first shock came when the Iron Curtain was dismantled, and I got a chance to come to New York, to Columbia University on an invitation as part of my student exchange graduate studies. My family stories of America and my personal long-time fascination with New York since my father's stories, now were coming to life. I opened my eyes wide enough to see all that with what I could fall in love: sunshine every day, instead of gloomy cloudy skies and cold weather, bright colors, instead of monochromatic palette, people being kind and helpful instead of looking at me with judgment. And most of all, I was free from that feeling that someone is always looking from behind my shoulder at everything I do. I was offered a teaching scholarship and accepted, working hard at it. In school, I met a young architect, and felt like romance is just the air New Yorkers breathe. Life was so fascinating and in the moment, everything seemed exciting. Supermarket shopping was a thrill. For a girl from a monotone routine behind the Iron Curtain, the bright side of life showed irresistible. I got married, and decided to make New York my new home.

### Pulling the Rug From Under My Own Feet
Wait, there is more!

As I applied my hard-earned degree by beginning a career in architecture, I soon realized that architecture wasn't for me. Now that I lacked the constant and nagging support of my parents in that decision I could not sustain the decision. What happened to me?

I took a small job in the waiting of my professional licensing to come through, while I was in transition. The job was at the drawing board, back then they didn't have computers do all the drawing like they do today. I was sitting at my desk one morning, drawing small changes in the repositioning of the bathrooms in a new hospital, sharp pencil in my hand, and an architect's ruler in the other, hearing the quiet murmur of the other people's rulers and pencils on their drawings, and... feeling nothing. I looked at the woman sitting at her desk next to mine, rustling her pencil against the paper of her drawing: fuller figure, grey hair, glasses. I looked at the pictures of her grandkids on her desk, she was very proud of them. I knew this wasn't my permanent place, and that soon I would have a nice and cosy job at a consulting bureau and a steady paycheck. My parents could only dream that I would make it so well so soon. But I couldn't wait. I have no idea what happened in that moment. It felt like I blacked out. Suddenly, I felt dread toward the work I can't relate to. My father was fascinated by architecture and I watched him do his work well into the nights. He always talked about it and looked forward to a new day of creativity. He loved his work. I watched my mother be the only one who worked during lunch in her bureau. She loved her work. I did not love my work. I did not love my profession. I did not even like it, I didn't feel anything about it. I was dead for architecture. I realized then that I had made a mistake. That Ph.D. that I earned - it wasn't for me. It was someone else's life, and I was not the right person to live it. Without thinking, I stood up, grabbed my bag and walked outside into the sunshine. I decided not to go back.

You can imagine the stir it caused with my parents. My father took my abrupt quitting architecture as betrayal of his professional loyalty on top of family values and social norm. "You don't just walk away form the 9 years of school, and all we gave you!" he exclaimed over the phone. I could not hear him. His words did not register with me.

My husband, also an architect, and his family didn't take it lightly either. He didn't expect such a move and insisted that he married an architect with a Ph.D., not an unemployed seeker I became. His parents, having thrown a large party for their friends on the occasion of our marriage could not see me in their life anymore. All they saw that I turned their life upside down. Well, this was the end of my American marriage.

I stayed in New York, and in the next few months I searched for a suitable career. I needed the money and a place to live. Going back to Russia wasn't an option. I did not know what I wanted. But I knew I did not want to go back. If I went back I would definitely be chained to the drawing board. I would work under my father's wing, and probably marry soon, someone he would choose for me from the inside his circle. Now that I didn't work out in America, back in Russia I would not be respected, and considered politically damaged. My title would be taken away. I would need to resort to either a low pay research assistant position, or a drawing board job. Dreading both of those opportunities, I contemplated my next move. I wish I had a plan or knew how to make one. I could draw a plan for a building, but not for my life. I had a PhD and yet, I knew nothing about making decisions in the way that I wouldn't regret them again. Just like that, overnight, I became my parents worst nightmare.

### Decisions, Decisions....

Decision time came yet another time and I really wished I knew what to do.

Do you know how you make decisions? Do you have a strategy how to make a life-changing decision like this?

This was probably the first conscious memory when I was truly puzzled, *how* to know what I wanted. I was used to following people who I believed had the authority, people who knew what was best for me better than I could know for myself. Suddenly, I was on my own, unaccustomed to having to make choices for myself. My choices were increasingly confusing, as I was not well equipped to make high-quality life changing decisions. I was 26 years old.

### New Beginning... New? Really?

I decided to apply myself in the field of finance. Money and security were the motivation. My organizational skills were suitable, I had enough boldness, good looks and youth and landed a position with a future at an investment bank. Simultaneously, I was accepted into a business school. Excited with the new world, within a year I found myself traveling internationally, pulling in a six-figure salary, which provided me with a comfortable lifestyle on the upper west side of Manhattan.

Finally my parents were proud of me. Do you know this feeling when you hear from your parents that they are proud of you? This is all great, but is this really what we live for? What about appreciating yourself? Do you appreciate yourself?

This continued until at the age of thirty-two, I began to question my choice of a "successful" career for the first time. I looked at the Statue of Liberty from the office window and thought about my work at the bank that occupied seventeen hours of my day and most of my weekends, that I was in charge of people, projects, and numbers, that I had important friends, privileges, and obligations, yet the esthetic flow, congruity, and dignity were absent from the life I was leading. I was pushed down inside and muted. I had my soul bagged and put away for years. I could buy everything I wanted: shoes, diamonds, antiques, dinners, first class flights to Paris, or London and I felt empty and uninvolved. I was good at what I did, but I wasn't happy about it. I had the money, but it could not buy me a peace in mind. I longed for something more, deeper, more meaningful. I felt dead inside. A dreadful thought occasionally came and went, with its prickly feeling, that Wall Street may not be for me. In the morning, I woke up with a feeling of disgust and I could not tell what it was or where it came from. I began to question myself and the choices I had made, but I still did not know what I wanted instead.

I looked at myself in the reflection of my window. On the outside I was successful, well organized, and incredibly attractive. On the inside I was unhappy, doubtful, and felt ugly.

Do you ever have a feeling like inside you there is another person who is the real you, and that person is hiding?

A part of me was pushing to be heard. I wanted to scream about how terrified I was about my life. I felt lonely, alone in my gilded cage, unable to see deeper and find the meaning of all this. I was leading a double life of outer success and inner lies. From beyond the window's reflection looked at me sad, lonely, overworked, and insecure young woman with my name. I called out my name: "Is it you?" I could not recognize myself.

To keep myself functional, I ate a lot of high-calorie food. I drank. I started to notice my body changing, inflating with every passing year, making me buy larger clothes. By then, I was 6 ( six!) sizes bigger than I am now. I just thought, it's aging, justifying it with the stress level and hectic schedules in my work, I would just go out a buy new clothes every season. Do you do that? Do you say to yourself, ahh, this dress no longer fits, to the back of the closet! A reason to go shopping, another temporary excitement. I felt uncomfortable with my body and with my lifestyle, uncomfortable with myself. I felt sorry for myself.

My stress level took its toll. In my early 30s, I began to rapidly put on weight. I did not have time to walk to the store, sitting at my desk for hours, so I ordered clothes from catalogs, upsizing to accommodate my weight gain. One day I was standing in front of a mirror, trying on the pants that had arrived in a box. The pants made me look ridiculous, bulging in the front with those stupid fashionable pleats. I shook my head at my reflection, looking pregnant when I wasn't even dating anyone, and burst into tears.

This had to stop.

Yet, I could not stop.

I didn't *have* to stop.

I was living in compromise I wouldn't give up. I spent money on clothes, shoes, collectibles, and vacations. I found temporary excitement in those things, and although I saw other people in my position doing the same, it did not provide the joy of fulfillment I wanted in my life.

Then it dawned on me. Even though I was out from under the influence of my old country and my parents,

I was still gaging my success through their beliefs and values, which rang hollow for me. All along I was trying to prove *to them* what I could.

My lifestyle wasn't meaningful for me. The clock was ticking inside me. It was time for me to experience the meaning of my life, the purpose, the deep appreciation of the fact that I am alive. I wanted to appreciate my life.

Don't misunderstand me! I valued the skiing I did in those years, and the places I saw during my world travels, the quality food I ate and the thrill of people I met and transactions I made. I appreciated living bright and big, I appreciated that all. That period in my life was invaluable. It gave me insight and sprang me to the life I have now. Then, I wanted to understand how to set my intention in life, how to see the value, how to live beyond consumption, how to create depth in my relationships, how to know appreciation in the moment... I did not have the tools to see beyond the price tag.

Working on Wall Street, after architecture, I switched careers, not values, I switched the industries, not the philosophy, I switched the doing, not the being. And it's the being that needed to be adjusted.

How about you? Are you aware of your being, purpose, intention? Do you appreciate where you are in your life?

I wanted satisfaction. I wanted peace, settling, grounding, relaxing. I wanted to come to rest about my life. I went on, not knowing what to do to generate satisfaction in my life. I didn't even know what it meant to have satisfaction. I still didn't recognize that I wanted satisfaction, meaning, depth in my life.

Suddenly I realized that I wanted my life to mean something to me. I wanted to know that I mattered, and I knew I wasn't accomplishing it at my job as a banker.

"If I die tomorrow - to whom will I matter? What has to happen so that I know I lived? How can I become happy?" I asked myself.

Perhaps, my life was someone's dream, but it wasn't mine. I still had no idea what my dream was. I was forced to confront the emptiness of my life.

I decided to quit. Like a decade ago, I wanted to walk away. I needed to find my soul.

I was thirty-eight years old. My search for the meaning of my life had begun.

## The Truth

*There are only two mistakes one can make along the road to truth;*

*not going all the way, and not starting.*

—Buddha

Which one is truer when you close your eyes: you sitting in a chair or you day-dreaming of being at the beach? I was stunned how real my imagination of being at the beach was. As I close my eyes, the room in which I sit dissolves, and I taste the salty breeze and feel the heat of sunshine on my skin. My feet are dipped in the coolness of the sea-wave, and in my hand I feel the dry hot grains of sand. As I wonder if I could get a sunburn this way, I began to realize that imagination, our mind's perception and belief are very powerful. I couldn't tell where I actually was: in the room or at the beach.

Just at that moment a blurry transparent angel appeared in front of me. I am still a banker and I am still very much for analysis and science, yet I was stunned how real my present reality is. A totally different world! It was barely a flow, a shadow, a vision, just a wisp, an awareness of a presence. The angel's name was Michael, and his red dress had an elaborate golden collar, not unlike an orthodox icon image which I had seen plenty growing up in the old country even though brought up *atheist*. The words *guardian angel* appeared, and a feeling of love sent to me overwhelmed me. Tears came to my eyes. This is the real truth: unconditional love. Floating in space with me, with no awareness of time, let alone a room or my status, was an angel and he was real.

I thought, that I am going bunkers. I must be tired or ate something bad. Suddenly, I felt a *pull* of my right sleeve. Someone was pulling my sleeve to get my attention. I turned my head, while on the outside I knew I was motionless. That motion of turning my head was very smooth and easy and I was immediately aware of what I perceived next. A smiling and giggling youth in a long toga with black short hair in disarray whispered to me that I had to stop being so serious and have fun and play. Right now. I wasn't not convinced. He then *showed* me the feeling of suspended rest, when my body and mind became completely light and free, when the only thing that matters is that this lightness and freedom continues.

I took a chance. Taking the angels' recommendation, I decided to take time off work and packed my bag for a trip to Europe. This was in early September, 2001.

On September 11, 2001, while traveling in Europe, I came down from a day's adventure to have a pint at the local pub. Sitting comfortably with my Irish Guinness and stew I stared blankly at the news on TV showing fire, alarms, crying and running people, and the collapse of the twin towers over and over again. Still not yet believing my eyes, and not realizing the scale of what I am seeing, I began to think of the people in the towers, who I knew and with whom I worked, but may never see again. I felt surprised and awed at the thought that if it weren't for the angel who pulled my sleeve attracting my attention to taking a vacation I would have been one of those running, falling, dying... By some miracle, I wasn't there. I was saved because I listened. Now I knew that *this* was the time to do what I wanted to do for such a long time. I knew it was my call to action. With that event, my life as I knew it—just like the lives of many others—ended. My adventure took a new turn. I came back to New York and submitted my letter of resignation. My spiritual journey had begun.

# A Story Is Alive

> *If we choose, we can live in a world of comforting illusion.*
>
> —Noam Chomsky
>
> *God is the experience of looking at a tree and saying, 'Ah!'*
>
> —Joseph Campbell

The work with my inner wisdom prompted me to embark upon a new perspective on life.

Spiritual guidance always comes forward to give wisdom and guidance; often we just don't listen. As I work with clients in higher awareness, the information emerges rich with metaphor, personal symbolism, and creative imagery based on the cultural backdrop of their pasts. I help uncover the meaning and personal symbolism of the discoveries in relation to everyday life and the future.

A metaphor is a story or an image that is symbolic of a larger meaning. An angel is a metaphor for a messenger or a guide, depending on the culture. Angels are not necessarily religious symbols. In fact, what I do has no relation to religion unless my clients initiate it. I work with the metaphors and symbols that comprise my clients' belief systems.

Metaphor is alive in narrative descriptions, images, or emotions and the transfer of associations from one context to another. Each client comes to me with a well-developed set of beliefs that are represented by a rich symbolic vocabulary of allegory and analogy that fits his or her individuality and reflects his or her upbringing and inherited beliefs.

As I work with a client, he or she visualizes his or her guides in accordance with his or her culture. For example, Sheila came from the Native American culture, and her guiding mythology was expressed as a hawk and a wolf, whereas, Nina, coming from a Christian background, subconsciously invited Jesus and the Virgin Mary.

In my unique work, I don't suggest the imagery to be used, seen or imagined; it is initiated as an emerging form from my clients. My role is to create the space and hold it so that the client can have the experience he or she wants to have. My expertise is in keeping the client secure and focused on the inside so that the client's story is free to emerge and take him or her deeper into that experience so that he or she can make the core shifts necessary to free him or her from limitations.

These expressions are rich with imagery based on what the client has learned previously, seen before, or know works for him or her. I find metaphor work very effective because its language resonates the most with our unconscious.

The people who come to work with me are willing to tap into the unknown, are stepping into their journeys of personal spirituality and self-discovery, and are committed to participating fully in their experience.

It is one thing to be told about yourself by another person, as in the case of a psychic going into trance and telling their client about what they become aware of regarding the client's past or future. Many of my clients are uninterested in the idea of others telling them about those experiences; they want to be in the experience themselves, feel, see, and hear the gusto of the light, energetic creation and they want to personally make the connection with those energies and guidances. Many had tried therapy focusing on understanding problems and instead want to focus on taking control of what they can do to make their lives better, shake off the constant presence of a problem, and experience the possibility.

Within the spiritual work I do is an implication that letting go of time, space, personal beliefs, and conditions, as in a creative metaphor of past, parallel or in-between lives allows us to do. The higher consciousness state indirectly parallels the life of the client within another fantastical time in a metaphorical format, when a similar situation was uncovered. There we find patterns of behavior that the client seeks to incorporate. Identifying those patterns and bringing them to conscious awareness is what I call "lessons learned," and the energy associated with the issue becomes free and available for conscious use. Temporary suspension of belief, ordinary reality, and the usual patterns of everything you know leads us to uncover a non-ordinary parallel reality and within it an awareness of what needs to happen for transformation through love and light.

# Psychological Benefits of Spiritual Work

*Education must provide the opportunities for self-fulfillment;*
*it can at best provide a rich and challenging environment*
*for the individual to explore, in his own way.*

—Noam Chomsky

*Psyche* is the Greek root word for soul. The Jungian concept of psyche is self. I deem this helpful in the development of normal, healthy individuals dealing with the challenges of everyday life and who seek meaning and spiritual growth, and the development of their daily decision making. In no way am I trying to represent this as a medical model or a psychotherapeutic model; this is purely practical and philosophical and may be intellectually stimulating, provocative, and entertaining, and it is definitely transformative and positive in change.

This spiritual work has powerful positive results. Whether I work with an executive, corporate employee, entertainer, or stay-at-home mom, the benefits of the spiritual experience are unique and worth experiencing. Let me highlight some of those benefits for those who are curious about why they should experience the wisdom state.

- *Experience Wisdom, Guidance, Eternity, Knowing*

The emotional availability arising through a significant meeting of spirit guides and experiencing their wisdom frees up memory, emotions, and direct access to such a connection to spiritual wisdom any time at will.

- *Experience Flow*

As channels open up and instant ability to access heightened creativity becomes available, you experience the desirable state of "flow." You are at will to do the things you are capable of. You find it easier to make decisions and act upon them. You shift from being a seeker and come to rest where you can raise your level of satisfying output.

- *Awareness of Limitlessness*

As a result, your preconceived notions about limitations are exposed and released. Connecting with your power, your self-esteem is elevated tremendously. You realize that you are limitless, completely without limitations. You realize that you can have whatever you want, and you understand that it is up to you to make that commitment.

- *Eliminate Fear of Death*

One of the major benefits of this spiritual work is that it allows you to completely strip yourself from any fear of death. Quite simply, through spiritual awareness you travel to other parallel existences and experiences of death, separation from the physical, and rebirth. This is an exciting experience. Living through death in a spiritual experience brings peace and transforms the concept of death. Finally, you experience your eternal soul without having to physically die. In spiritual research about "past lives," or "in-between lives," emotional pressure to know the ending eases. Metaphorical "dying" precisely reveals information about previous lives in your own words; unlike hearing a stream of images from a psychic, you are in the experience firsthand and receive the information in an embodied form. Rather than just being intellectual, this experience contains information for all your senses.

- *Experience Freedom to Change*

Useful patterns of new behavior become apparent and take hold. If you decide to repeat the old pattern of behavior, you will be internally reminded of the consequences. You have absolute choice and autonomy from an internally driven position. You can act or choose to do nothing. You are able to make any choice, including being free to create a new, more powerful story.

- *End Necessity for Secondary Gain and Making Excuses*

Another major benefit of spiritual work is the removal of secondary gain. Many people get stuck in negative patterns because they receive an unconscious benefit from the ineffective behavior (e.g., remaining helpless so others will take care of them). The inner realization allows the secondary gain to dissipate as the motivation to move forward increases. Clients report spontaneous relief from discomforts that had previously persisted over long periods of time.

- *Make Higher Quality Decisions - The Ones You Don't Regret*

Perhaps the most significant benefit of the work we do in higher consciousness is setting up the new kind of decision making. At one with your higher consciousness and with guidance, you experience deeper meaning and a kind of knowing where everything seems doable, possible and obtainable. It is then, when you begin to dream big, spread your wings, and with a new sense of direction, purpose and intention, you leap freely to your desirable experience of what you really want. Transcending limitations the decision becomes clear as day, as well as the next step to it's fulfillment. This assuredness of the decision they are making is what most people want and don't know how to get. And this is what I found is the most beneficial consequence of the work that I do: to help you develop your ability to make better, higher quality decisions.

## Role of Imagination—Is What True?

*Every myth is true one way or another.*

*It is true when understood metaphorically.*

*But when it gets stuck in its own metaphors, interpreting them as facts,*

*then you are in trouble.*

—Joseph Campbell

Our human mind is very powerful. Imagination is a vehicle delivering the necessary pieces of information to the decision making stations in our mind. We pay attention and pick the ones we need the most and imagination plays an extremely important role in connecting the dots in narrating of our journey. This is also significant when we use our imagination to perceive a future or the past, in real or projected events, people, ideas.

Neuroscientific research emphasizes the way we explain to ourselves the reality of our world through our perception.

What is real? We contemplate being on a beach as real then move to being in the room from which this projection happens as we sit in a chair, then move again to the reality of the beach experienced in a deep, profound three-dimentional way. All doubts about that reality go away, as we consider that reality is what we perceive as real.

Extreme importance plays the mental position from which the imagination reenactment and recall happens. Whether we are in a positive or negative mood, subsequently we remember good or bad memories, and we might have a pleasant or not so pleasant experience. With time going by our memories of the past fade, like dreams after awakening, leaving us with a sensation associated with the event, that we assigned to it, and true facts become touched with our attitudes and desires when we represent them to ourselves. Keeping this in mind as we create our own story, the narrative we tell ourselves and others, of the past or a future, becomes a reality.

We are the only species that is able to imagine what is not there (in religious experiences, for example) or give meaning to symbols, words, and images. Each person has his or her own unique perception of universal symbols that mean something very special only to him or her. We often downplay the use of vivid imagination as being childish, but we behold successful innovators as being visionaries. This is a direct contradiction in our westernized society and only serves to discourage those who could make viable contributions to the world if given the encouragement.

If we can create a real world, why not create a world that is beautiful, supportive and successful? Why not let go of the world that is disturbing, disempowering, alarming? Why not believe in the reality that is a loving, supportive and creative? Such reality exists. All my clients experience their reality that is tangible, creative and free and come away with a way to connect with the depth of meaningful existence.

In our sessions I lead the seeker to their wisdom state accessing the depth of the person's inner world through their subconscious. The primary language of our subconscious mind is metaphor, symbol, and picture, whereas the conscious mind's properties are in the spoken language, numbers, and written words. Sometimes conscious judgment leaks through, and the thought comes: *Is it true? Am I making this up?*

Set the judgment aside and continue the process. Experience yourself inside the journey of your life and enjoy the experience. Allow the imagination to create a world of possibilities regardless of whether it makes sense or not. There is plenty of time to prune back the ideas once you begin to take action.

So now let's take a look at the neurobiology of my work.

## Brain Science Behind My Work

*When we quit thinking primarily about ourselves and our own self-preservation, we undergo a truly heroic transformation of consciousness.*

—Joseph Campbell

Often I encounter skeptics who want scientific proof before they can accept the validity of the metaphorical references in our work. Coming from a family of academics, I was curious myself. Current neuroscience is grappling with these concepts and finding some very interesting answers. The main question still remains: *is what we imagine true?* Is the wisdom you experience in the spiritual awareness a true experience? Where do those profound revelational experiences come from? What is behind the revelations, imagination, perception of inner reality?

With these questions in mind, a few years ago I embarked on a neuroscientific study that conclusively points out that meditative states have psychological, emotional, and physical benefits. What I have come to discover are much more than just facts and benefits.

I studied the neuroscience that hypothesized and researched the logical connections between creativity, memory, awareness, and higher consciousness.

Early prominent psychologists determined that the mind adapts the concepts and beliefs we form in early childhood into a vocabulary of personal representations for easy interpretation of situations and to dictate responses to our environment, creating a complex vocabulary of personal symbology for everyday use.

### Neurobiology of Stress Consequences

Bare with me as I delve into some science. It is important that you read through what discoveries were made in recent times regarding stress, and the importance of the mindful work with your inner wisdom in managing a healthy living. Recent discoveries in neuroscience show how the perceptions of the outside world influence our inner awareness and subsequently can influence our physiology, creating health.

Our responses are based on the filters we created as we developed. Research shows that responses that are triggered by certain situations, people, voices, words, images, sounds, and smells can be purely primal and based on old memories. In my work, I help others through their transformational experiences of conscious awareness and assist in creating structural changes in these perceptions of themselves, essentially reorganizing the filters through which they perceive the world.

In daily life, we actively perceive information through our senses—our skin, eyes, ears, noses, and tongues. The data goes to the receptors of the central nervous system. Through the sensory channels of the central nervous system, the data is delivered to the brain. Depending on the quality of the data coming through the receptors, the neurons fire off special chemical components into the bloodstream, identifying the quality of the data and creating the experience of perception.

If a person is afraid, under stress, and in struggle, the body responds by releasing stress hormones—epinephrines—triggering the production of catecholamines—chemical components of the bloodstream that thicken the blood in initiating a fight-or-flight response.

In the brain, special neurons fire off, making synaptic connections with the limbic system, and in it—the amygdala, our primal brain, and the first "resource" on the checklist for safety and survival. Furthermore, the "data" is processed and released toward the hippocampus, evaluating the importance of it for survival, triggering memories, and imagination of consequences, then further to the prefrontal cortex areas, anterior cingulate cortex, where the "meaning" is assigned, emotional responses are initiated, and future memories are generated, detailed and evaluated, then decided upon, and reasoned according to other memories of "self" that are stored deeper in the limbic system. Then, upon completion of this process, the action is triggered. No action is also an action, so when the "waters are clear," no action, sitting back and relaxing *is* a proper action.

Forty-thousand years ago or more, when we lived in the wild, we adapted to have this response in place in the case of a sudden attack by an animal or other foe. Our distress was always temporary, and once the danger passed, if we survived, we would return quickly to neurological equilibrium.

Today, stress is ubiquitous. So is the stress response. We are used to being wired and tense. Most of what we are afraid of is invisible and long term. So we remain tensed. Fears of losing our status in the forms of work or money, family concerns, and fear of aging and appearance act as perennial phantoms that trigger the primitive fight-or-flight response. There is no escape and no abatement. Many people find themselves in stress overload and adrenal fatigue, which means that their adrenal glands are exhausted, being constantly under pressure producing adrenaline, and unable to supply the necessary adrenaline that motivates us to take proper action accordingly. By now it is well known that stress repercussions can be seriously damaging to our health and have long term echoing effects.

Both long-standing effects of living without mindfully letting go of muscular tension and effects of stress lead to many diseases and accumulated illnesses. The leading theme of a person's life becomes survival, in which the only desire is to stay alive, not *feel* alive.

Meaning is made as a result of filters set in place through an inner set of beliefs stored as memories of behaviors and through a narrative available to the individual from the middle area of the brain. During our work together the inner physiological circuitry is facilitated to fire off the "understanding" and "connection" back to the frontal areas of the neocortex. The brain creates a "vision," a personal "reality" according to the individual's views. Corresponding with the input, suggestions, intentions the person's view begins to form on his or her place in the universe.

From a position of pure survival, according to Maslow's hierarchy of needs, the response will always be a pure response to the question, "How can I get what I need?" This is the physiology of stress.

### Brain Science Behind Gamma State - A New Perspective - How Can I Contribute?

In the work I offer, I show how one can experience the other end of the spectrum. In a relaxed and focused awareness, a position of balance allows a person to experience positive elevated consciousness, view his or her role in the universal scheme of life, and see his or her place in the universe. It is of this position spoke Joseph

Campbell in the first function of mythology: "A myth is meant to reconcile an individual to the experience of awe in relation to the divine in his or her life."

In balance, physical calmness, and equilibrium of the mind, the creative decision-making process becomes possible as opposed to pure survival. The physiology of balance allows for a more "wholesome" state of mind, in which both the rational and intuitive abilities of the mind are optimally available.

Rich in serotonin transporters, prefrontal areas of the brain—particularly the orbito-frontal cortex—activate the associations and reward-based cognitive connections with the limbic system, and again, if in balance in a higher consciousness position, in, what I call, gamma state, solutions emerge.

The gamma brain wave, which entrains the brain in a particular way and is achieved in higher consciousness state, stimulates the connections between areas in the brain responsible for *creating* future memory and *taking action* toward the decision that is identified as the most adequate. The new neural pathway quickly fires off in the new direction and thus establishes a new way and possibility.

This enables the seeker to connect with a metaphor of his or her personal role in the universe. Subsequently, connecting the dots according to the intention, a creative action emerges as a solution, a strategy of the next step, creating an active inner vision of necessary action to be taken in the near future.

In my work, I utilize protocols that allow quick access to the gamma brain wave. Gamma state is a highly intentional state of mindful self-awareness, implicated in resolving the binding problem, the essence of which is *how does consciousness of perception form*?

The metaphor of unity of "me" in relation to the "world" is well known in neuroscience as a sensation, and it occurs when a particular part of the brain is stimulated to awareness. Notable evidence was discovered in gamma research that explains the clearly heightened sense of consciousness, bliss, connection to god, and deep intellectual acuity in and subsequent to *focused* intentional meditative states.

Besides tangibly improving physical health, letting go of stress, relaxing the body, and oxygenating the brain, while in a safe and comfortable balanced awareness in gamma state in a controlled environment, a client's physiology experiences massive amounts of oxytocin—a natural hormone present in states of a heightened sense of well-being. In gamma state, the individual experiences pleasure from connecting with his or her spiritual guides, attaining the information, and sensing a harmonious place in the universe.

By stimulating specific areas of the brain in gamma, one has the opportunity to gain insight, wisdom, and knowledge about his or her place in the world and the community and awareness about his or her life's purpose. When you establish a connection with the inner wisdom as you remain in this state during your session, new neurology activates to further strengthen your ability to use optimal brain function to project possibility into the creation of positive outcomes in the future.

After the session, clients return to their day-to-day experiences with the knowledge of what to do and the ability to relax deeply, and they continue to be open to the information that deepens their knowledge about what to be doing through time to create the future they intend for themselves, with expanded mental ability and improved decision making resulting from the new access to neocortical brain function. As a result, they are literally building connections to use more of their brains for higher-quality decisions in everyday life.

# Wisdom II: Pursue Your Bliss

*Follow your bliss and the universe will open doors where there were only walls.*

—Joseph Campbell

## Do What You Love

*Do what you love.*

*Don't do what you don't love.*

*If you do follow your bliss you put yourself on a kind of track that has been there all the while, waiting for you, and the life that you ought to be living is the one you are living. Follow your bliss and don't be afraid, and doors will open where you didn't know they were going to be.*

—Joseph Campbell

I left Wall Street when I found myself confronted with a "now or never" opportunity. I revisited my background in mysticism and spirituality from the old country. My soul began to come out of the closet where it was hidden for many years. I had to fall asleep in order to wake up, when I took a deep interest in skills in hypnology, positive self-suggestions and neuroscientific research about the power of mind. I began to experiment with mindful approaches and "alternative" practices including Hypnosis, Reiki, Reflexology, Aromatherapy, Polarity, Tai Chi, Neuro-Liguistic Programming (NLP), branching out to hand and palm analysis, Wicca, Tarot, and delving deeply into brain sciences like neuro-biology, sociology, psychology to help me understand the intricate working of the universe of our consciousness.

In 2001, after I left banking, I developed a hyperthyroid issue. Once at the doctor's it was suggested I would probably have to take thyroid medication for the rest of my life. I was basically healthy until that moment. So I didn't find the idea of getting on a thyroid pill for life particularly appealing. My mother and my sister-in-law were taking that medication. I wanted to take a different route. Little did I know that pursuing an alternative solution to an illness would change my life so dramatically.

When crisis occurs, I am not usually the one to panic. My father says, "You must have a warm heart, a cool head, and clean hands." I think this came from his childhood spent in exciting times after the communist October Revolution in Russia. Now was the time when I could really appreciate the saying.

A girlfriend of mine claimed that she beat breast cancer by doing something called Reiki. I called her up to find out what it was about. She pointed to her Reiki teacher. She said, "Take the class, learn to do it for yourself and then just go for it. This stuff works." I found out that in order to use the technique, I had to experience an attunement with the universal energy field, and the next *yearly* class for such experience was the upcoming weekend. It was a clear opportunity, and I signed up. I knew an omen when I saw one. Remember, I came from a mystical culture…

About the same time I discovered self-suggestions and

hypnosis. I was curious about directing the power of the mind, creative visualization and self-training. So popular back in the early 70s in my old country, it was now back in fashion with me. For the next three months, I walked around holding my hands to my throat, murmuring my mantras for health and energetic restoration. People saw me acting weird like this; I didn't care. I wanted my life back in control. Once I bumped into an old girlfriend from my banking days in the street who mimicked the position of my hands at my throat, and asked what I was doing. I told her what I had been instructed: "I am doing Reiki for healing, it is a new old medicine. It's the pure energy from the universe that flows through my body—a channel for this energy, into my hands and out to a sick area in my body. The intelligent energy changes molecular structure to heal that spot. Add positive suggestions and affirmations." The girlfriend said, "I see, as you left the bank you went completely off the track. You are a sad story," as she walked away. I didn't care. I wasn't sad. I worked very hard, applying positive thinking and carefully crafted mindfulness suggestions to myself using self-hypnosis and neurolinguistic programming. Like I said, I wanted my freedom, my health, my life back. I had just a few weeks to achieve it, because the next testing was in three months. You know how sometimes you are really committed to something you chose, and you just plow your way through to the end to have it come through? Have you ever done a project where it was your idea and you just *wanted* to do your best. You *know* you have a great idea, and you *know* it is going to work. You have no doubts; you just don't allow yourself to doubt, because this is your chance. You are constantly moving forward, looking strictly ahead, never behind, keeping focus at your task. You are *in the flow* and nothing can stop you. That's how I was.

Three months later when looking at my tests results,

my endoctrinologist raised his eyebrows and then asked, "The tests are normal. I am curious, what did you do?" I said, "Reiki." He sent me off without listening to the end of my story; there was no sign of the ill condition, and that was mystifying to both him and me. Him because all I had to say goes against his medical degree, and me, because I suddenly realized, that there is more to reality than what we see.

My further experiments were bringing results. I was intrigued and started to study all that was interesting. I certified as a Reiki master and completed a professional certification as a hypnotherapist, plus a number of other certifications, including NLP, storytelling and transformations of personal mythology. I wanted to share what I had learned with others, and soon I opened the doors of the New York Awareness Center, a community of self-awareness for healthy New Yorkers. I have worked with hypnosis for stress, bad habits, low self-esteem, poor self-image, and childbirth. As I developed my philosophy, I moved toward spiritual hypnosis phenomena. I began to offer personal mentoring work to people with whom I felt a connection, to whom I had the most to offer, and who appreciated my work with them. In the last ten years, the New York Awareness Center has become a center for those seeking meaning in their success and deeper purpose in their lives and for those who want to be more effective and balanced in more areas of their lives.

I do what I love. I do what I know to do well. Every day I wake up, and I am glad I made this choice. I appreciate the community of people who provide me with work and who are interested in deeper learning.

This does not mean that I don't make choices anymore. Every day I choose to continue to do this work, and I choose it over other work I could be doing. I choose enjoyment, I choose fascination.

# Pursue Your Bliss

> *One way or another, we all have to find*
> *what best fosters the flowering of*
> *our humanity in this contemporary life,*
> *and dedicate ourselves to that.*

—Joseph Campbell

Remember the movie *The Matrix* with Keanu Reeves' character Neo?

Neo was just a nerdy computer programmer, devoting his time to figuring out the matrix he uncovered. Other than work on the computer he knows little else in his life. There is this unfulfilled longing, dull repetitive routine of his life, undesired tomorrow leaving him with yearning for something more.

One day he was sitting at his computer and his phone rang. He was jolted out of his routine, and invited to meet Morpheus who offered to start a mysterious adventure under the name of figuring out the Matrix, for which Neo must choose: the blue pill or the red pill. The blue pill will allow him to go back to his dull life as it was, the red pill will signify the beginning of a new exciting journey into an unknown world. Morpheus says, "You may survive, or you may die; there is no way to know. But you will have a time of your life." Neo chooses the red pill.

Like Neo, I offer you this choice now. Take "the blue pill" and you will forget this choice. You will go back to your old life the way it was, with its dull routine and longing. Take "the red pill" you will go on a journey of your life, see the truth you yearn for—an adventure, totally unknown, totally unexpected. The adventure will make you feel alive, energized and fulfilled. You will have a sense of purpose, meaning, and the satisfaction of having lived this life with intention. On top of it all, your existence will make a huge difference in the world.

I invite you to make this choice.

I, like Neo, chose the red pill.

Which do you choose?

The choice is simple. Yet it's not easy.

The following are stories of a few of my clients' experiences, who also had to make choices and some of them did and some didn't.

## Lisa's Story

One of my clients was Lisa. Lisa was a forty-four-year-old executive working at a major radio station. Her questions were about the next step to choose in her career. She had been in her current position for the last twelve years, and she was bored. She was seeking to spice up her life but didn't know how. She was living "with her eyes closed" and having difficulty finding joy. When she reached her wisdom place, she leaned to her right and "looked" toward the right wall as if she "saw" someone there. I saw her eyes moving under her closed eyelids. She was having a conversation with someone in her mind.

Lisa was thinking of quitting her job. The lesson from her source of her wisdom came to her, and she conveyed to me what was being told to her:

L: No more working at the desk as a chore. That's what is being said to me now. Further, the work becomes what you love to do. The desk is pushed out of the picture. I still see myself staying on the job; I just do it differently. I feel myself differently …

M: What's the difference?

L: I am more mature, intentional, and more fun. I am fun to be with, and I am having fun.

M: How do you do that?

L: I smile. The point is not what I do. It is what I do with the energy when I do it. It's how the energy works. I have to let myself be in the light, and there is so much light … It feels so good. Letting myself feel good in the whole idea. Ha-ha. After all, they say you are not here not to feel good.

Lisa left with a sense of having received a complete set of instructions from her guidance on how to be in the light so that her energy and attitude would change.

## Eliza's Story

Eliza, forty-eight, called herself a photographer and a songwriter. She had just had her third baby and was successful on the outside. Yet she wanted clarity on her life's purpose. She felt confused about what she should put her attention toward. When she connected with her guidance, she asked her question.

It took her a long time to get the response from her guidance. They didn't answer her in words. Instead she saw animals, nature, sunshine, flowers, and people laughing and dancing in nature. I helped her navigate. I asked what it meant to her.

M: What should you do with this?

The explanation came quickly.

E: It's the world of life. All around me is life. My guide is a wolf. He transmits to me the knowledge. I don't have to do anything to know; I just know. I am a teacher. I hear words, "You are a teacher." I ask, "What do you teach?" "A plentiful palette of creativity." All my favorite things: writing, songwriting, poetry, creating a place, a community for people to come, a workshop place near the ocean, working with women following their hearts, empowering them.

She continued.

E: I have another guide standing at three o'clock to me. It is a crow. He said, "Don't forget about the 'magic' that comes from the inside of you, ability to travel between thresholds. Keep yourself prepared. Wear your power jewelry. Eat light food. Keep your body toned so you can perceive the signals in the environment."

M: What is the most important thing?

E: Commitment to your path. Without commitment, you can't accomplish anything. Focus must be on your intention. A lioness is at my feet. I am not afraid, although she is big. She puts her head on my feet. She feels like my grandma, Isis. "Remember that you are strong," she says. "Powerful internally, courageous like a warrior. You are prepared for leadership. It is time you take the lead." Now suddenly I see her as a woman with a buffalo horn headdress. Centered, more connected, flowing throughout my body, rooted deeply in Earth.

M: Who are you?

E: I am a golden light, like a warm fire inside with lots of colors—blues and greens, some pink and yellow. I see triangles, some pointing up, some down. They are flowing around me. They bring love, lots of love.

Later, I explained to Eliza that symbolically triangles symbolize male (pointing upward), which is active action, and female (pointing downward), which is flow and creativity, energy. Energy of active flow creating love was key for her new ways of being. A confirmation came from her next guide—a dolphin.

E: At four o'clock, dolphins appear, childlike energy, play. Have fun. Play. Be like a child but not childish. Don't be afraid to move around! Don't take things too seriously! Smile! Stop worrying! Be more trusting. Just let go. Your new baby is a way for you to stay creative and flowing. I feel energized as they infuse me with energy. Charged. The energy comes from the sea, like a liquid fire energy. Tapping into the source of creativity and purpose.

M: Where do you experience this energy?

E: Impulse of energy is from the bottom of my belly. Upward and surging, springing me upward. It feels joyful and exciting, empowering, refreshing. It is good to feel my physical body. They are sending me more energy. They say meditation can be done physically. I ask how. They say, "It is like this." I feel energy going up in my body and then downward and upward again. Cleansing at the same time as healing. Like the ocean washing me over, down and up again.

M: Ask them to take you to where you can ask your questions.

E: Now there is angelic energy, kind of like Jesus surrounded by angels. I am not a religious person, and I don't know much about Christianity … but here they are with their young androgynous faces.

M: What is their message to you?

E: We are all one. There is a sea of light, and I am walking on its shore. The purpose is to live my authentic self and to help people become more aware of themselves. Doesn't matter where I do it. Life choice, intention, and fulfillment are not really a choice; they are more like an opportunity to participate in the unity consciousness and make your mark."

M: Ask how you can fulfill your purpose better.

E: You are already doing it. "Listen," they say. "Stop worrying. Listen to your intuition. Stop thinking that it's wrong. Take good care of yourself. You will need this body for more. Do more of what makes you feel good."

## Kate's Story

Kate, forty-three, worked in a corporate environment as an attorney for a large bank. Kate was a successful executive and suddenly found herself devoting her time to researching the meaning of life. She took a look at her future self. In her session, she accessed a complete future memory of the woman she wanted to be. Happy, smiling, standing tall, in better physical shape—in front of her stood the complete image of her future self, who already had what Kate was looking for: meaning, purpose, fun, love, and creativity. Speaking with the present self, her future self gave her guiding suggestions:

K: It does not matter what happens on the outside,

what shiny objects are attracting your attention. You have to learn to use the energy. Then you can have anything.

As an attorney, Kate pursued further clarity, asking for concrete description. How could she acquire the ability to "work the energy," and the advice from the wisdom poured in.

K: Work out, eat well, get the "stick" (the visual metaphor for exercise and balance) to use with energy (the metaphor for life). That will help you align your energy, have more fun, do what you love to do, keep doing it, step into the swirl. If you focus on the swirl, it will get bigger. Right now it is too condensed, too strong for you. If you levitate with the stick, you will make the swirls bigger, looser, not so rough, less intense so it sweeps you gently. Part of it is to stop putting yourself behind others, fitting in, trying to fulfill the other people's expectations of you before you decide that this is what you want.

As Kate approached questions about her career and clarity on her decision, the guide spoke through her to her higher self.

K: Regarding career, work, job, it is not for us [guides] to point what you choose to do. Focus on what you love to do. Make space for that energy. Do what you love. From there, live your life sharing your space. Then when you are ready, you can help people and share your life. How you get there is what's important. And something will click for them. It is all important.

She experienced a sensation of completion and satisfaction and a profound sense of well-being. At that moment her guides told her the following:

K: All other questions on your list are not important. There is really nothing else for you to know at this point. Go home and live your life. It's not a question of doing more; it's a being. Only be from this position of balance.

Kate clarified.

K: If I keep asking questions, I will keep needing to know about the past or something else. I need to move out of this mode. You can't get relief by knowing the answers because there will always be more questions. Put them down. Look away and look forward to what's ahead. Have fun. You are always living in your intention. Be aware of this balance, whatever your life's intention. Is the feeling of doing it right for you? Bring this spirit in. Have an experience of your life.

## Marcia's Story

Marcia, fifty-four, was looking to enjoy retirement from banking. Now that the kids were grown and she and her husband were left to enjoy each other, she was learning to re-experience herself in the next stage of her life. Similarly to Kate, Marcia's guidance was to learn to have fun.

M: It's time to let go of seriousness. It is time to be myself and laugh and have fun. It is the simple joy of connection. Even if you think it is really hard, it is not so hard. It is easier than I ever thought. I feel so connected now. Now I can pick things to do that I like to do with my time. Oh, it's so easy to enjoy myself by myself now. I had forgotten that, but now I am reminded about what I am about, what I like.

# Wisdom III: Be in Balance

*Participate joyfully in the sorrows of the world.*
*We cannot cure the world of sorrows, but we can choose to live*
*in joy.*

—Joseph Campbell

## Balance

*We see things not as they are,*
*we see things as we are.*
—Chinese Proverb

One of my clients, Lolita lived by the sea in a suburb near New York, and her free spirit was well suited by her chosen career as a set designer in the entertainment industry. However, in her thirty-eight years she had not developed a good method for making decisions. Her sure fire method was to write down pros and cons and then more pros and then more cons until she just went a familiar route to pick the thing she felt more comfortable with at the moment. The problem with pros and cons was that depending on the state of mind she was in, she found either more pros, or more cons. When she was tired and agitated she was likely to find more cons. It's easy. The world seems to be against you when you are agitated, didn't you notice? When something good was going on, or on a Saturday morning, after a swim, she usually felt great and life seemed good, so she found more pros. She usually took a chance on her decisions, many of which she admittedly regretted afterward.

Recently she got married to a man her parents "approved" for her, having been already involved in an ongoing affair with her boss who is married. She said she just took a shot at the marriage, because of the expectations from her parents, to see what happens, as she just couldn't decide how to or whether at all to end the affair with the boss. She felt confused and torn. She did not want to hurt anyone anymore and she felt fed up, but had no method of making such life-changing decisions. So we asked her spiritual guidance to help.

As she reached her place of connection with her wisdom guides, in the light, the advice came to her quickly and definitely.

L: The guide says to me: Can't decide? You are not in the position of making a decision. You must do it differently, they say. You are missing a step. First there is an important step to find yourself; that is you in balance and in peace. Find your balance. Balance is first. Then decide.

Lolita became adamant about finding from her guides how to be in balance. They explained that there was a way that was unique for her, and it was a universal way to balance herself. Every time she needed balance, she could start by doing it this way.

L: Go to the sea, go to the beach, walk around, feel the breeze, sit down, grab some sand, throw it in the water, spend time looking at the sunset, remember love, breathe, let go of hurt, open your heart, create love.

There was a valuable message here. When she was growing up, Lolita's freedom was important to her, but in her household with seven other siblings, the rules and limitations had been set. Lolita had to behave in a mature, responsible way before she got a chance to be childlike. As a young adult, she was gone with the wind at the first chance. Her creativity was often interrupted to attend to others. Her inner sense of herself was tucked away and muted. With adolescence her sense of freedom came from doing things in spite of the rules, or advice of others, and often in spite of herself. Her creativity and nonconformity made her a successful set designer, yet in her personal life, creativity was challenged by the lack of maturity and sense of accountability. She had to learn to give up her childish behavior, and she had to choose balance to be able to handle the responsibility. Now she had to learn the difference between being childlike and behaving childishly. This was the real choice. Was she going to take the challenge?

With a sense of balance, Lolita could now make a decision she could not make before. There was a long silence. In that moment, she not only had to make a choice, she had to stick to it. Only then her life would begin to make sense. In that moment, with balance, the commitment became possible. Instantly, a new way of making choices became a possible alternative to a shot in the dark. Lolita was thrilled with the new wave of opportunities about living her life. She didn't have to feel like she was missing out on anything by choosing one. On the opposite, now she was looking forward to direct all her focus, her energy and her creativity to one choice and make it work.

The guides did not tell her to make that choice. They rarely tell you to do a particular thing. They just bring you to a point where it becomes clear to you that this is the thing to do. And then you can choose to do it or not to do it.

The guides revealed to her how full her life could become if she devoted herself and her emotions to one focused relationship. They showed her how much creativity could arise from taking the energy previously wasted on hiding and calculating ways of preserving personal safety and redirecting it to creativity within one chosen relationship with certainty, just like when designing her sets she knew exactly when it was complete and was satisfied. She wept emotionally at a possibility of a new way of being and made her commitment to remain a childlike, joyous personality with responsible, mature behavior to make her life easy and hold herself accountable for her decisions.

## My Magic Will Go with You

*If I had a world of my own, everything would be nonsense.*

*Nothing would be what it is because everything would be what it isn't.*

*And contrary-wise; what it is it wouldn't be, and what it wouldn't be, it would. You see?*

—Lewis Carroll, *Alice in Wonderland*

Sometimes my partner, Mark, and I find it relaxing yet stimulating to take walks around the city, along the Hudson River, or through Central Park. Spending time in nature, I find a renewed sense of vision, which encourages me to stay in balance when I return to work.

Astonishingly, the perspective from which we view our world and from which we create meaning depends on our physical condition. If we are fatigued, mentally or physically, maintaining balance can be challenging. Thoughts and sensations can become internal saboteurs. A few deep breaths, physical stretching, a short nap, or a brisk walk can reset our physical bodies and our minds back to a perspective of positivity, searching for opportunity and sense of well-being.

The attitude we choose as we tell our stories changes the quality of the narrative. It also changes the trajectory and sequence of events that emerge from a new, changed story.

One of the journeyers with whom I worked during my recent visit to Israel, Dana, wrote that she felt that the "magic" she had experienced during her exquisite spiritual travel in my presence had left with my departure. Dana was thirty-seven, single, and quite successful at her career as a computer designer. Last year she lost a close friend, and consequently, she developed a series of "bad" habits that seem to stifle her self-perception, take her time and made her "feel bad afterward". After I worked with her for a few hours, she experienced what she described as a "magical awakening" from living inertly and being a "frozen popsicle."

Sometimes people identify with ideas, images or actions they take, and they forget that they are not their ideas, beliefs or their past. They are alive and they are themselves. Only recognizing that life is a fluid motion of energy one can begin to partake in a process of change. Dana became aware that she was "amazing and magnificent" when she was just herself. She sat there, absorbed, eyes closed, quietly attending to the awakening of her self-awareness, witnessing the process with a renewed sense of experiencing her physical sensations and a subsequent sense of well-being. The experience on her face changed from worry frown to a peaceful glee. She commented on experiencing the letting go of an enormous weight of her trauma, and her sense of loss was replaced with a lightened sensation of peace. Her body seemed to know what to do to align. I held the space for her to regain her awareness. "Magic" happened inside her.

The next day, she let go of the magic. She was confused. One moment it had felt so good to be her, and in the next moment it was back to stagnant energy of the past, guilt, and regret. I placed her awareness on her own discoveries and her sensations when she was in balance.

I quickly pointed how to notice that the "magic" was still there. The key was to allow herself to keep focusing her attention on the magic inside instead of *defaulting* to attending to where the magic was *not*.

It is true that it was easier for Dana to concentrate in my presence because I direct her attention. I pointed to the pattern of how she generated this sensation for herself. It was so easy for her to focus, and it felt so good that she perceived it as magic coming from me, outside of herself. Like most people, she found it difficult to believe that her experience was generated by her, not by me. Initially, it was facilitated by me; I have been a catalyst of an important focused point in her experience because I directed her focus, but essentially, and I emphasize it to her, that she was the embodiment of her way of being. Without her participation I could not have achieved the result she had created. She is the essential part, I am just the catalyst, a specialist trained to see what about her, that generates the light, and is hidden from her own eyes, and point it to her.

She experienced herself in a well-formed and balanced way. This experience is sacred, very personal for her and, of course, memorable. Her body and mind, her entire being came to rest. She experienced equilibrium, the connection with her truth, tranquility in her busy mind when it let go, and her wisdom instantly became present. Suddenly she knew how she was when she was alive, and she felt profoundly "alive." She whispered, "I feel alive inside!"

The inner spiritual intelligence became present and manifest.

Dana experienced her life energy rising from her pelvis to her solar plexus and her chest, opening her heart and emanating outward. The energy was permeated with colors: purple, orange, and yellow. As the colors changed, they radiated to various parts of her body. As she described her sensations, her eyes watered. In this moment, she felt fully alive.

## Magic of Staying in the Light

Dana perceived it as me performing "magic" to help generate a desired way of being until she could do it for herself and on her own. Simultaneously, I gave her the tools to promote the kind of flexibility and alternative choices of ways to create and sustain the "magic" until she became able to make connections on her own. A name for this state is *balance*. Staying in balance is staying in the light. That's a starting point.

Dana learned to identify and sustain her position of feeling alive. Experiencing her "ah-ha" moment helped her to subsequently generate better thoughts and positive beliefs about her perception of herself.

When she spent time experiencing herself in the way she wanted to be, it was helpful to her because it helped her create a different future. In that moment, she began to open up to the possibility of generating a sense of well-being on her own, which helped her to essentially change her story, her own belief about herself, from *I am not enough* to *I am myself*.

Subsequently, organizing her life in the way she wanted it to be became possible. Her perception of herself, her abilities, and new possibilities arose instantly. She needed to continue to work on sustaining that creativity in order for her to *consistently* generate this feeling as a new default. By a new default, I mean a new way of behavior in which every time she is *not* in the position of balance, she would *make a choice* to recreate that balance with the perspective of the desired intention for her future, defaulting to the *new* behavior each subsequent time. Upon working further with her over a period of time that she determines on the basis of a desired predetermined tangible result in her life, I would set up opportunities to act as a driver for necessary changes in her perceptions until she can do it on her own.

## Binary Position

> *To know the true reality of yourself, you must be aware*
> *not only of your conscious thoughts, but also of*
> *your unconscious prejudices, bias and habits.*
>
> -Unknown

Balance does not mean only being relaxed or static all the time. Not does it mean to be emotionally flat and unable to feel or see the other position. We are human beings. We get off track sometimes. It is normal. Knowing how to get back to the position of balance, from which to begin again, is key. Being in balance allows a stable way of being, from which it is easy to hold a perspective of possibility and creativity while simultaneously disallowing and eliminating inhibitions, limiting beliefs, and problems. It is a binary position; one is either in an opportunity or in a problem.

As mammals, we behave in a similar way to animals, which can only be in two states: (1) relaxed and energized in search of food or a mate or (2) wounded or pursued, scared and seeking shelter, safety, and survival. This concept of two opposed perspectives has been well researched by many scientists and pioneered by T. Grandin in *Animals Make Us Human*: "*My theory is that the environment animals live in should activate their positive emotions as much as possible, and not activate their negative emotions any more than necessary. If we get the animal's emotions rights, we will have fewer problem behaviors... All animals and people have the same core emotion systems in the brain.*"

Like animals we are binary in our position. We cannot hold two positions at once. If we are sad, we cannot be happy in the same moment. If we are happy, at the same time it is impossible to be sad. So in order to be in one position, it is necessary to leave the other. It is the experience of ourselves when we are in a state of possibility as opposed to being in a problem state. Physiologically, it is impossible to be in both states (both a state of possibility and a state of problem) at the same time.

Simplified, our experience is always binary like this: we are either in joy or in fear.

In joy, light, and love, with singing in our hearts, our creativity is on the rise; we are in love with the world, and we are connected to innermost and highest intentions. We are able to access deep levels of energy and come up with our best solutions. In fear, we are busy trying to survive, putting one foot in front of the other, barely looking up, scared, and uncreative. Now, logically we apply this idea of binary position to ourselves in order to obtain desired results. A fearful employee cannot be creative, and a joyful person is not easily discouraged. You choose where you want to be.

## Role of Mentor

> *Most people are not looking for a purpose,*
> *most people are looking for a feeling of being alive.*
>
> —Joseph Campbell

Sometimes it is very hard to take the first step on our own. We need someone who has walked the path, someone who has what we want, and someone who has the necessary training, emotional availability, and personal depth. A person who lives what he or she teaches. This person must have walked the path ahead of us, know the way, and be able to offer to hold the space for us until we can do it on our own.

Back in childhood, that person was our mother or our

primary caregiver. As adults, we need someone who is a voice of wisdom, another person who can be a trusted adviser. Not a friend but a professional who can guide the serious conversation we need to have with ourselves and who can lead us to the right answers, not give us the answers. Someone who leads us to the position in which the right answers become possible when it is time for us to begin to have serious conversations about meaning in our lives.

In ancient cultures, that was the role of a shaman, an elder, or a teacher who could pass on the rite of passage to a young and immature adult and facilitate the opening of the channel into future adulthood. Today in the western culture, we have lost the ability to facilitate transition to maturity, having eliminated the step of the rite of passage, informing and training the youth, teaching and giving them adequate tools for making personal decisions. As a result, the majority of the population remains in a stage of "young adult," without the ability or a facility to step into adulthood. That is why we have so many young single mothers, obesity, and irresponsible behavior about personal health, money-related decisions, career choices, and relationships. When they come to their thirties and forties—and sometimes their fifties and even sixties—people find themselves seeking the meaning of their lives and their purposes, unfamiliar with their desires, body sensations, and internal wisdom, and they are unable to make a leap to personal accountability for their experiences.

Over the last decade, I have devoted a lot of my time to working through what is meaningful for me. I have done so with my mentor, Joseph Riggio. Even while teaching others, I never stop learning. I don't believe anybody ever does.

It has been discovered by neuroscientific studies, and contrary to popular belief, our brain displays inner plasticity and we are able to learn new information and adapt to new ways until we are deep in our old age. During most of the 20th century, the general consensus among neuroscientists was that brain structure is relatively unchanging after a critical period during early childhood. This belief has been challenged by findings revealing that many aspects of the brain remain agile and changeable even into late adulthood. Decades of research have now shown that substantial changes occur in the lowest neocortical processing areas, and that these changes can profoundly alter the pattern of neuronal activation in response to personal experience. Neuroscientific research indicates that experiences can actually change both the brain's physical structure (anatomy) and functional organization (physiology). Neuroscientists are currently engaged in a reconciliation of critical period studies demonstrating the immutability of the brain after development with the more recent research showing how the brain can, and does, change.

Dr. Richard Davidson of California Institute of Meditation Studies showed in 2008 that contemplative meditation helps create new neuronal pathways leading to acquiring peace and mindfulness in meditation which helps deepening life meaning. "Mindfulness - moment to moment non-judgemental attention and awareness. We can change the brain by changing the mind," said Dr. Davidson.

That is a new way of perceiving self-evolvement for humankind. Change your belief, and the change in your life is imminent.

The challenge is in finding that position from which it becomes possible to make a decision to give something up in order to gain something instead.

As to my client Dana, there were a few things she needed to do. In order to sustain the "magic," Dana's guidance conveyed that there were some changes Dana needed to make.

Sometimes people are not able to make a change or

take a leap right away. When I worked in the corporate world, I wanted pleasure bestowed upon me. Hundreds of shopping trips, spa treatments, and vacations later, I still was not able to find peace, satisfaction, or contentment, and I continued wanting more, longing for meaning.

I was unaware of my own responsibility to direct my attention to pleasure in my life, feel it, and live it and simultaneously and actively direct my attention away from displeasure. In professional language this double action is called *propulsion*. Don't just separate yourself from what you don't like, also create active movement toward what you want.

For this you have to, of course, know what you don't want, don't like, don't desire and stop associating with it, be it people, work, or, what's most difficult, behaviors.

And what's even more important, you must become aware and know what you do want, desire, and wish for, the result you are going for and the value you place on it.

To organize this propulsion, we all have the responsibility to ourselves. No one can or able to make us step on the road to creating the desired result in our life, it is our own decision and doing. And that't the most incredible part.

Incredible because in a way it is freeing to decide to step into the path of a journey.

I did not know this responsibility was mine not someone else's, it was my decision to begin to make it happen. When I became aware of the concept of accountability, it took me some time before I could "man it up," commit to it, and assume it as mine. Transition happened when I worked with my mentor, from seeking the experience done to me to being ready to be in the experience I created for myself.

That was the time I was ready to work with the guide, my mentor, my teacher. Until then I was a seeker, trying on different hats with various teachers, theories, opinions.

I heard them, tried them on and spent time and money figuring out if *this is for me*. If I had chosen to work with a mentor from the start, I would have saved years of time and a lot of money by developing a *strategic awareness* of my own unmistakable decision-making process and knowing of myself much earlier in life.

In the work I do, I work with people—not applying my skill *to* them but working *together with* them—to lead them to the source where they can make their own adjustments. They feel safe and can make any adjustments they like because as they connect to the source of wisdom that is hidden from them when they are in a "problem." With me they enter into a space where opportunity for adjustment, change, transformation becomes possible. I help you find the place from which the source opens to you and gives you unconditionally according to your desire. Then I teach you the skill to sustain that connection for yourself.

There is an old proverb that reads, "Give a man a fish and he will eat for a day. Teach a man to fish and he will eat for a lifetime."

When you uncover your secret wisdom, it is not the end of the story. It is just the beginning. What you choose to do with it makes all the difference.

"You need only enter halfway into the dark forest before you begin to come out the other side," says another clever proverb. In other words, change your attitude, update your thinking, and a new vision emerges immediately and imminently. When you attend to the vision of a possibility, desired life changes begins.

## Create Balance To Stay In Balance

> *We can be sure that the greatest hope for maintaining equilibrium*
>
> *in the face of any situation rests within ourselves.*
>
> —Francis J. Braceland

Erica, forty-nine, was a quiet woman with little confidence. She called herself a musician and a composer, working in the corporate world to pay her bills. Her desire was to fulfill her passion in music, to be more powerful, and to be worthy to be respected by others. Eventually she wanted to do music full time and bring to the world the esthetic pleasure of the music she heard in her mind.

Her inner guidance connected her with the awareness of the power and wisdom she already possessed. From there she was able to determine what she needed to do to build the future she wanted for herself.

Erica acted as a channel in the conversation between me and her guides about herself in the third person. Her guidance gave her direct instruction talking to me about her in third person.

E: She should stop putting her attention on temptations, toxic behavior, or thoughts. Stop indulging in self-pity. That's damaging to her music. She needs to focus on love and exercise discipline in that focus. She should keep herself in shape and exercise; then more soothing music will come. She should be thankful for the environment. She has accommodations, a home, and food, and she doesn't have to worry. Now, she should just focus on music every day in every moment. She should be grateful for everything all the time and have more confidence in her music.

M: How does one have more confidence?

E: She thinks she can get more confidence from the outside, from someone or something else. The main thing is that she is not really sure that she is doing the right thing. What she needs to do is sit up straight and stop slouching. It's a bad habit, and it hurts her intention.

Erica turned her head to me, her eyes still closed. She spoke at me as her guides used her channel to speak to me.

E: You [Morrin] must tell her she needs to be in balance in her body. Posture is important. Posture is key.

Straight posture creates a different sensation; it creates different thoughts. Bad posture is toxic behavior. When she slouches, she is indulging in sadness, lamenting her situation. Get rid of it, sit up, strengthen the support, and start riding the bike.

It is not the first time the notion of upright posture has come up in conversations with wisdom guides. There has been conclusive and evidential research from movement experts Frederick Matthias Alexander, Moishe Feldenkrais, Thomas Hanna, and Paul Ekman, along with others, who have developed theories indicating that physical alignment and micromuscular sequences affect our moods, our thoughts, and our abilities to make decisions. These attitudes affect our actions, the actions affect our character, and our character affects our destiny.

We rarely are able to observe ourselves, and our own behavior. A guide, a mentor trained in it will be able to point out to you what your body does when you express some of your thoughts and beliefs. *"Belief is a matter of customary muscle tension,"* F.M. Alexander's descriptions of physical body responses in regard to our thinking process might come as a shock to most of us.

In the work I do, these principles play an important role. It is not unusual for me to hear a guide's direct suggestion like, *"Sit up straight,"* to know that my client is on the right track.

What is amazing is that wisdom seeped through from the depth of Erica's unconscious into Erica's awareness while she was connected with the spiritual guides, and brought directly to her attention.

Furthermore, Erica's guides pointed out to her that duality is essential to recognizing whether you are in balance.

E: We must know dark to see light. It doesn't mean we work with the dark. We need to make a decision to only work in the light. Finding balance allows us to cut through the darkness. Balance inside the light is so easy. Balance is light.

This again points to creating the balanced position. Once in balance, sadness and limiting thoughts go away, allowing for the sense of well-being and creativity.

## Healing Happens In Balance

*Healing is a matter of time, but it is sometimes also a matter of opportunity.*

—Hippocrates

Joanne, forty-five, wanted to find relief from her neck and shoulder tightness. It was important to her because she was a professional artist. As a painter, she needed her body to be in perfect physical condition to create large commercial murals in her Long Island studio.

During her wisdom journey experience, Joanne was guided to a "balance room," and her guides asked her to rid herself of a persistent feeling of guilt and a feeling that she was "missing out." Her issue was that she felt like she was missing out on life.

As an artist, Joanne was doing what she wanted. Ten years ago, she worked in banking and was very successful as a private banker. She managed to save up enough money to quit her job and start a painting business. She created murals for private schools in Long Island and in Manhattan and for private collections. She had reached new heights in her artistic expression in the last few years and was working on placing her paintings in a museum.

All the while, she was carrying a tremendous feeling of guilt that there was something she was missing out on in another life, in the banking career she had left. She felt that her life could have been different, in some ways more or better. The grass is always greener on the other side of the fence.

Her guides instructed her that if she let go of her guilt as she had been instructed, as of that very day, she would not suffer any more. They also instructed her that her "healing" would depend on her perspective and intention and her direction in the future.

Healing of a physical body was interesting to me for many years, ever since I started the New York Awareness Center, because I created healing for myself. When I became sick with a thyroid issue, I made it go away using the techniques I presently use. I began to identify how the healing occurred.

The position from which one approaches healing makes a huge difference.

People often ask me to help them heal their issues, their karma. In many people's eyes, healing is about making issues go away, getting rid of pain, and looking into past patterns so as not to repeat them. In other words, healing is about ridding oneself of problems.

This position is limiting.

How will you know that the issue is gone? How will you know that you will never repeat the behavior that brought on the original issue?

I found that work from a positive bias is faster, easier, and more in alignment. When situations are viewed from a position of seeking opportunities rather than finding limitations, I call it a positive bias. When in balance, in alignment, it is natural to be looking out for opportunity rather than for limitation.

When in alignment within ourselves, when in balance with the intention and with our desired future in mind, there are no issues. If there are limitations found from a position of balance, they are viewed as simple stepping stones on the way to results, something to work on, and they are overcome with intention.

Sometimes we find ourselves in seemingly unpredictable situations. Many report their surprise with being dissatisfied about how their health or relationships or careers are going. I explain that there is no issue, just a current situation. It is not unpredictable. It was predicted years ago when they made a first decision leading up to their situations today.

Many want to know their past lives, experiences when they had similar issues, and the cause of the problems. If approached from a position of pain, karma, and self-pity, the answer only inhibits the limitation. How we got here is less important. Knowing the cause for the "issue" does not mean that we have skills to create solutions. Looking at situations from a positive perspective, with intention for the future in mind, opens a series of ways to find solutions. There are no issues, only current situations to be resolved going forward. There is no past, no pain to move away from, only future and ways of going forward toward it.

When a person is in balance, there is only the present, no past and no future. Take a moment and just experience the present—the breathing, your muscular tension and subsequent relaxation, the sounds of life around you, the pulsing of your own bloodstream in your fingertips.

Create a position of balance.

When the present is experienced from the position of being in balance and in alignment with yourself, your idea of the desired life arises from a different perspective. Your future seems clearer, the intention for the life you want becomes more defined, and a possibility of the desired future with clarity arises. Having established an intention and direction supports only one way of movement: movement toward it.

Once a person enters into a place of wisdom with balance, there are no issues, pain, karma, or past. It is all gone. The place of wisdom is the place of learning and knowing. There is no need for healing. There is just a letting go, a realization of having this now and then moving onto the next moment: now this; what next?

All fear is released, all doubt is gone, all darkness

is dissolved. There is only light, balance, and certainty about who you are, where you are going, and what the best way to get there is. This certainty dissolves the unknown, and the unknown becomes a known reality, predictable and malleable.

There is still stress from the job, need to support the status, kids, etc., but the point is that once you are in balance, there is nothing to heal.

One can argue that being in balance is an attitude. To support the balance, one's attention on the actions that need to happen must be in a particular direction. Each person can generate balance on his or her own by realigning the body and redistributing his or her weight, whether sitting or standing, to create symmetry, balance, and esthetic movement.

Arising is only the positive, exciting expectation of the life ahead. In that there are some decisions to be made about how to get there, and that's all there is. Decisions about the future from a position of balance become very easy.

There are only things to expect and be moving toward. Progressively, I developed clarity around healing as a "moving away from issues" strategy. Essentially, healing is a negative bias strategy. Healing presumes that there is an issue and that there is a need to get rid of the issue.

Another more effective strategy is, from a positive perspective, allowing access to wisdom through balance. This strategy allows the creation of a future from the point of now, not from a point of the past. When in balance, as a strategy, it is easier and clearer to begin developing steps that allow us to move toward the future we want.

When I learned this model of accessing wisdom from balance, my work became even more exciting for me and, of course, for my clients. Now we spend less time researching what went wrong in the past; issues of emotional, tragic, and dramatic responses; unsatisfying past lives; limitations in spiritual development; and pains of bad decision-making strategies. Instead, we access past experiences and past lives only from a positive bias from which we can learn the lessons and find out useful success strategies used by their souls in their in-between life journeys. We spend more time connecting to the wisdom of creating the lives they want; perfecting the access to a sense of freedom, strategies of better decision making, satisfaction, and contentment; and defining direction, intention, the legacy they want to leave behind, and ways to fulfill themselves.

I knew exactly what Joanne needed. She needed to learn to be in balance, to be in the light. From experience, I knew exactly what her guidance would be doing next. We had to get to work on her finding balance. Sure enough, as soon as she reached the light, she experienced relief.

J: Being in the light is such a relief. Layers are being peeled off of my essence. I am becoming pure, clean, and clear. In itself it feels so good. It is relaxing, and it is refreshing. I thought I wanted healing. I am already healed. It happens so quickly. There is nothing to heal. I am already forgiven, and I already let go. There are many people to forgive. Now it is my turn to forgive. Let go of guilt. Somehow as soon as I ask, I have it granted. I feel I am free from karma. I have let go of karma. Funny, as soon as I say it, it is gone. I let go. I feel I know the lessons I had to learn through the karma I had. As a spirit, as a soul, I feel the ease with which I would be released. As a human being I feel that I get lost. I have to remind myself to be generous and grateful and to see the world from the other side. Let go of tension. Let go of the past. Be at peace. I experience love and quiet and a sensation of peaceful excitement, hope, and curiosity.

M: What is a good reminder for you so you can remember to stay in peace and be in balance? Ask your guides to give you a key to it.

J: I will be reminded with a sound in my body. It is a vibration. It is a pleasant tone.

Suddenly she spoke in a changed voice. She spoke in second person, directly addressing herself as her guide.

J: We live in a matrix. You are here, doing the living and being here in the wisdom place, at home. You choose the living. Combine it now with the life of your choosing and make choices here and now. The matrix is simple; it is like a hologram. The choice is to allow your mind to follow the structure of peace, love, balance, purity, and present and only that. You can re-enter the matrix and make another decision. Live in the present, not in the past, not in the future. It is all one: only present. There is no past or future; it is only present all the time.

Her voice changed to her own again.

J: They are showing me a super-view position. Everything moved away, and I am elevated above, and I see the grid. I can see the matrix!

Then she went back to the guidance channel again.

J: Look and see. Love is purity. Matrix is only making sense when you take a super-view position. You can see how pieces fit, what numbers mean, and how the life makes sense.

She was herself again.

J: Wow! It all makes sense now. I don't even have to know because I know that I already know. And that's enough. I can move on to do what I have to do next.

Before her session, Joanne had questions about her relationship with a significant other. She had vacillated for months on the brink of leaving the relationship, which was tenuous. She felt it had reached a moment where something had to give. I knew this was the right moment to ask her the next question.

M: Ask the guide to give you advice about your partner.

J: You can't live on the edge. It is being out of balance. Either stay or leave. Do what you want and let go. Commit to one thing. Focus. Can't have both. Love and pain can't be together. Leave one.

M: Which one do you choose?

J: I choose love, compassion, and peace.

M: Sounds like you have to commit to it.

J: I commit. I know this is the right thing to do.

M: What is the attitude with which you approach your partner now? See yourself do it.

J: Full commitment and love and now I can feel so much love, as if the gate opened up. I am totally and completely focused on this love.

A month later I received a letter form Joanne thanking me for the work we had done. She now enjoys being in a place of balance as her life moves on.

## What Is Balance?

*The best and safest thing is to keep a balance in your life,*

*acknowledge the great powers around us and in us.*

*Live that way, and you are a wise man.*

—Euripides

The first time I became aware of a concept of balance was in my early thirties.

I was paying little attention to areas in my life other than my work. Balance—in my family no such word was used. What was used was the idea of hard work. Just like my father, I believed that I needed to work hard all the time. I came to an absurd position: If I wasn't working hard, I considered myself lazy. If I wasn't accomplishing, I thought of myself as unworthy. I tried to utilize every minute of the day.

Even when traveling for pleasure I exerted myself, waking before dawn to walk the foreign towns until I saturated myself with impressions. I never gave myself time to enjoy the sensations the views evoked, just checked them off the list of visited places. At work for seventeen hours a day in the office, whether it was necessary or not, I was the last one to leave, making sure there wasn't anything else to do in the office. And there always was more work. Finally, I found myself out of balance. Working many hours a day, eating more than necessary just to keep myself alert, not allowing time for activities like resting or exercising, I quickly put on weight and was unhappy with myself. I had to change something.

It took time to discover the effective methodology that helped me regain my balance for the first time in years. My life shifted. As I rediscovered who I was when I was most myself and began to live my life from this position, "magic" began to happen in my life. Miraculously, the universe began to assist me and created circumstances for me to find love, romance, and pleasure that I hadn't been able to find before. I found what it meant to be myself, living from within and enjoying life with intention, which really led me to begin to look at my work differently. It was a long and fascinating journey from then to today when I no longer say, "I have to go to work." Now I say, "I don't work." I wake up to another day of being myself.

Having access to "magic" and creativity in my life allows me to be in balance in my desired position. Now I live to share it with the world.

# Wisdom IV: Relax and Feel Good

*The goal of life is to make your heartbeat match the beat of the universe, to match your nature with Nature.*

—Joseph Campbell

## Relax, Let Go, Feel Good

*Take rest; a field that has rested gives a bountiful crop.*

—Ovid

Many people coming to seek spiritual experience are stressed by their daily routines and situations needing solutions. When I begin working with a new seeker, I often find that the person's guidance suggests relaxation.

Relaxation is a way to balance his or her body and establish a connection to wisdom. In this person's spiritual journey, his or her guidance advises him or her to find relaxation as a means to restore balance. I have discovered that many people do not even know what it means to let go, let alone relax. Even if when they know theoretically, they don't usually do it or don't know how to apply it as a regular practice. Most people carry tension in their shoulders, necks, backs, and abdominal regions. Often our breathing is shallow.

Simply put, absence of static muscular tension creates relaxation. Physical relaxation slows down the brain activity, slowing down self-judgment and critical thinking, and creates meditative states, in turn opening the nervous system to allow us to be more receptive to learning, enjoyment, and pleasure.

By relaxing, we enter into a state of well-being. Deep breathing brings more oxygen to our brains and signals the nervous system to go into a "safe" mode. Blood circulation improves; the chemistry of the blood changes, allowing blood pressure to lower, improving the internal organ functions, and restoring health and body functionality. In relaxation, the gradual transition to a different level of brain activity translates into a change of mind, conscious perception, improved self-awareness, and connection to inner wisdom.

A change in physical sensations in the body changes our thoughts and awareness. Spiritual guides in almost every person's journey point out that because we are spiritual souls living as human beings, we are consciousness in a physical body, and we need to attend to our physical beings and keep them safe and effective so we can function better on the level of mindful awareness. In other words, keeping ourselves in a relaxed state leads to health restoration. In a healthy body is a healthy mind. Regular relaxation leads to clarity of perception and subsequent higher quality decisions, behavior, and action.

When our bodies are in stress, our human systems go into a fight-or-flight response, making us mentally and physically defensive. Automatically, we are programmed to seek security from the perceived danger, whether it is real or imagined. Our experience of stress, whether during the workday, in anticipation of or during an argument, or even while watching an action movie, over a long period of time, habituates our bodies to hold muscular tension even when we are unaware of it. In most cases, when the tension is not released, it begins to display increasingly serious consequences through physical, mental or emotional symptoms, such as digestive disorders, cardiovascular disease, allergic reactions, aches and pains, or emotional outbursts that threaten relationships, careers, and personal sense of fulfillment.

Some people resolve their stressful situations by escaping into distractive behaviors like overeating, dangerous addictions, and misbehaving instead of taking a restful, relaxing moment to enjoy themselves by slowing down their breathing and improving their body chemistry.

Being attentive to and relieving stress through regular relaxation and meditation exercises is imperative for a healthy, creative, satisfying life with intention. Developing the habit of releasing muscular tension is a necessary activity to sustain balance and health.

An easy way to relax that requires no props is described many times during the connection with spiritual guidance as rejuvenation, recharging the battery, or showering with light. This rejuvenation may consist of a simple breathing exercise; taking a deep abdominal breath creates a flow of oxygen to our brains and stimulates blood flow into various organs, creating a pleasant sensation in the physical body and a sense of well-being and peace in the mind.

When your body relaxes, the mind follows. When your thoughts come from a relaxed body, you are much more balanced. After just a few deep breaths your brain begins to think more relaxed, peaceful thoughts.

This is simple physiology. In spiritual sessions, the wisdom describes the physiology of relaxation metaphorically and often shows journeyers the way they experience themselves when they are relaxed.

This experience is anchored into the cellular memory of the seekers, and this further stimulates their nervous systems to open for learning. Accessing a powerful learning state is key to providing ourselves with an environment for better decision making and the creative potential for personal success.

So let's point out several important benefits of relaxation.

## Relax to Access Your Best State

Despite her analytical thinking, Celia, forty-four and a technology engineer in New York, was able to quickly access her guidance. Through her transpersonal connection journey, her desire was to confirm being on the right path to better fulfill herself in her capacity as a manager of a large group of people. She had a unique personal challenge to manage herself better and let go of her anger and impatience as a starting point to improving her management on the job. The first step was to learn to relax.

Celia accessed the wisdom and was silent for a while. Then she spoke the wisdom that was transmitted to her.

C: My mission is about love and gratitude toward myself and others. Before I can be grateful, I have to forgive myself. Forgiving myself means to let go of the hurt and push it out of my awareness. Bring forth my love. This is simple ... but not easy. They show it to me now. Rose petals are all around me on the white background of the cloud where I am. The cloud is for me to contemplate and meditate, away from distraction, to understand how to come back to my center, because it is all really about me. I have to change my attitude, become relaxed, let go, and stay calm. On the cloud there is nobody else with me. I own it. I own myself.

She continues.

C: Talking hands are caressing my face. There is more than one hand. Endlessly caressing me. Soft angelic wings. I ask who that is. They say they are here to comfort me and to help me let go and relax. I have to understand that I am free from bondage I imposed on myself. I set the lock, and I have the key. I am taking my ball and chain off, and like a bowling ball it rolls into the distance. Now I feel free. I feel good. It feels good to feel that freedom. My spirit soars. Something I am not used to. When I was young, a teenager, I always wanted it off, that ball and chain, but it seemed to always stay with me. This way, when it is off, it is better. No more worries, no more pain. Peace. Bliss. Mindless bliss.

A group of souls came in to greet her as she continued to feel free, in bliss.

C: They are asking me to let them in. There is a feeling of relief, and I let go. Freedom to have no more worries. My husband appears in a beautiful red shirt and talks to me. Our lesson is to nurture each other, forgive, and love. There was the greatest hurt, and he is sorry, and I forgive him. So easy. We have a few past lives together. Once he was my business partner and cheated me out of my wealth. Another one was in an ancient world, in Egypt. There he took care of my kids as a woman governess, and I was a man; my wife in that life killed him out of jealousy. My wife in the ancient life is my mother now. Oh my god! Now it all comes together. Why we have this convoluted karma. The guides say that they release my karma because I am aware of it now.

She became still with a peaceful expression on her face. Relaxed in her chair. Then she continued.

C: Now I feel peace and joy. A possibility to wake up in the morning like this, happy and at peace, another new day, opening to my journey, letting go of all karma, experiencing the knowing and the greatness of life.

When she reached the point of deeper wisdom, I

asked Celia to ask her guidance to show the future of her current life and what the relaxed attitude would mean for her position at work and for her life in general. She responded quickly.

C: I see myself in the future, powerful in a relaxed way. Yes, relaxed and then powerful. I can see myself in that way, relaxed, powerful, and I feel like it is me. There is energy in that relaxation. It is not being mushy or loose; it is being calm and light, relaxed yet energized, with energy softly surging upward from my root, up to my throat, making my breathing easier. The relaxed attitude is very natural. I feel that I don't have to sweat the small stuff or any of the questions. Seems I already know all the answers. Questions go away. I just know it. I feel I just know what to do. It is very easy and comforting. The knowing is so natural. I feel secure … grounded … emotionally stable … flowing … serious yet happy at the same time. I feel really good, really high, like I'm on drugs but much stronger, clear and empowered. I am laughing, surprised that I am so clear in my head. I am so clear and sure of what I need to do. I can see myself do all those things I have been putting off … I can feel the calmness. It is like a vast sea, the ocean, calm yet powerful. Deep and clear. This is the best feeling. I feel really good!

M: What can you do with this attitude in real life?

C: I can do anything! Absolutely anything! There is no doubt I can do things I need to do.

M: What about your anger?

C: I am calm, so I don't need to be angry anymore. When I feel anger come on, I become powerful like the ocean, and I direct my energy to create love and communicate clearly. I am very clear about how to do it and that I can do it. Will I do it? Of course. It is easy now that I know it. So there is no need to be angry. Everyone understands each other, and we know the common purpose of us being together. Easy to stay calm. What a great tool.

She thanked the guides for uncovering for her the tool of awareness in managing herself.

## Relax to Create Love

Maria, a thirty-eight-year-old executive from Long Island, commuted every day to do her business on Wall Street. She reminded me of myself years earlier. The stress level in her job was high, and she was looking to access a more relaxed quality of life. She was successful in her priorities, yet stress was taxing her body, inhibiting her libido, leaving her numbed, overeating, and putting on weight. Unable to be generous with her husband, she witnessed her relationship dwindling downward as months went by. As she relaxed and followed her guides' advice, she became aware of sensations in her body.

M: In a way, I feel tingly in various areas. I feel like my body lets go in various areas, and I feel it is not only physical. It is an emotional letting go. It's like layers peeling off an onion. It feels so good to relax and let go. Now my angels are here to guide me to relax more. Wait, can it be even more? Wow, I did not know I could relax more. I almost cannot move. Well, I know I can, but I don't want to, and I feel my body dissolving, melting. Wow, this feels so good. I wonder what use is to relax like this? I mean, I know there are benefits, but how can I be sure? Oh, they are showing me something … I am seeing myself relaxing on a beach in Hawaii. We were just planning the trip, and I was deciding against it. Peter and I have no time to relax. Wait, I am seeing myself on that beach, and I feel so good. As a result of this, they are showing me that my husband and I are in perfect harmony. There, on the beach, we make it happen. We make love. Oh my god! Like before when we were young! We both feel so close to each other. Rekindling our love. I feel so melted, relaxed, and in love. This must be good for me. I've got what I wanted. You can bring me back now,

Morrin, because I have to go home now and be with my husband.

## Relax to Clear Physical Issues

Margie, twenty-nine, came in the hopes to alleviate a bothersome skin condition. Her guides were very direct and clear with her.

M: Relax. Just relax. They are telling me to relax. There is a theme!

She laughed.

M: They are telling me to relax. They are telling me to relax because I always want to go someplace faster than I should. I can see how this relaxation clears my skin. My skin is so clear. The skin condition was present to show me that I expect too much of myself too fast. If I slow down my eating, eat right, relax, enjoy, let go, and smile, I will have what I want, which is clear skin. Eat right and relax, they say. Do the exercises and smile. Usually I have no time to smile. Smiling feels good.

## Relax for Pregnancy

Reina, thirty-five, was pregnant and wanted a session to spiritually connect with her unborn child. She was a director of research in a pharmaceutical corporation, and science and research were her passion, but her stress level was enormous, so her body had resisted conception for a few years. After a series of in vitro fertilization treatments performed by her medical doctor, she finally conceived and wanted to support her body in fertility and spirituality so her baby would be healthy.

Her guidance offered her a new template of behaviors. Almost in a bulleted format, she quickly recited them as they were given to her, and I wrote them down:

I.     Don't get angry. Anger empowers heavy negative energy. Don't retain any of that energy. Trust. All is well. Breathe. Relax.

II.   Don't be so hard on myself. I am doing a lot at the same time. I am a successful scientist, and I am becoming a mother. There is a lot to learn. First, learn to relax.

III.  Learn to let go. Let go of the past, which means to let go of each moment as it passes, not trying to hold on. Just let it pass. Relax.

IV.   Trust the letting go. Release. Breathe. Relax. If I don't trust, I might manifest illness. The voice is very loud. I have to listen. I have to follow. I have to relax.

V.    Instead of worrying, relax, bring in white light, expel the worry, release it, command it out, relax, replace worry with light, let go, fill it with light, feel the light, let go, relax.

VI.   Surround myself with people who support me, who have that energy of light. Just pay attention, and they will show up in my life. Relax. Stop the worry.

VII.  Don't let the negative thoughts get a hold of me. Realize that negative energy does not belong to me. Dissolve it. Bring the light instead. When I relax, the light will come. The light will tell me what to say, do, or think. It will be much easier that way.

VIII. Allow myself to let go of control. I can't control anything. Only myself. Have an intention. Control creates worry and desire for things to be different, and that sets off the disappointment. I am shown the stars in the sky, many stars, like a velvet blanket with diamond sparkles. Question: who do I think controls this? All I can control is stuff in my head. It is all illusion. It is all a veil. Raise the veil and I will see. It is easy.

## Relax for Creativity

Gina, a thirty-eight-year-old Italian pastry chef who enjoyed expressing herself at one of the finest restaurants in New York, was looking to apply her passion in a love relationship and create a family. She held herself hostage in loops of thoughts about limitations of her previous relationships without letting herself forget her "lessons." She felt "dry" like "a stale cake" that had lost its moistness. Gina's wisdom was all about relaxation. Her guides kept pointing to her stressed body and stifled creativity as a woman. They pointed out that all she had to do was translate her sensations in creating cakes into creating her relationship.

G: Relax, they tell me. Let go. This is lesson number one. They show me how I do baking. Like my hands are doing it for me. I've mastered that one. The sensation in a relationship is the same. I will know it is the right one when I can relax and feel creative. Until then, just keep trying. They show past relationships. I was hurt. It is the only thing I can remember. I have to remember the positive memory of when I felt loved and basked in love, relaxed and creative. I have to make room for the next one, refresh, restore my soul. The feeling is like being showered with love and light. After a while it feels like the whole universe loves me. I feel loved. It has a taste of sweetness to it, like the sweet smell of flowers. I feel love rising all through my being and splashing outward. The love is inside me. I am loved … by me. Loving myself is to relax when I am tired, rest, restore my strength—physical and emotional—respect my body and mind, and stop torturing myself with negative thoughts. I feel the pull to let go of the past, and it is so funny, tingly, and tickly. I feel the past hurts separating from my skin like an overbaked cake deflating, falling. Allow fresh flowers, dancing, the breeze of the ocean, the fresh taste of cool water in my mouth. Allow myself to just sit there and be showered with love and light. Hear the sunset. Can you hear? I can feel the sun dipping into the ocean … There are blooms opening around me like in the spring. One has a breath. I can hear a deep breath. Another has a light, bright light from the center illuminating all around me. Yet another has a feeling of love, the word *love* in big popping letters floating out of opening blossoms, very tasteful. This is very restful to enjoy these blooms opening and closing in a rhythmical pattern, and they remind me of my backyard in my country house. I have to go there more often and sit, watch, and relax.

She was silent for a moment and then spoke up again.

G: I just had a great idea for a wedding cake I was struggling with. Now it is all clear. I can see it. I can do it.

Gina experienced a flow of creativity in her connection, and her guidance revealed her next project and steps for her to achieve deeper professional success. She was satisfied.

## Relax for Clarity

Oreanna, thirty-nine, was a creative writer and a channel for angelic communications. She wrote a few books that brought her professional success. She wanted more clarity and deeper connection with her angelic guides. Her long light-colored hair streamed down her shoulders when she nodded to her guides in understanding.

O: As I talk to them, I am feeling energy in my hands, prickling, tingling, although my hands are very heavy. Now I ask, "What do I need to do about this energy?" I hear an answer as they speak one after another.

M: Would you like to share?

O: Sure. I don't need to do anything about it. Don't need to do anything. Just experience it. I have magic in my being, in my hands. It is just reminding me of who I am. A physical being. A magical being. All I need to do is to relax and enjoy my physical being. The rest will emerge from here. It will make me a clearer channel. I can access deeper information. I can see and hear better.

# Wisdom V: Have Fun

*The privilege of a lifetime is being who you are.*

—Joseph Campbell

## Are You Having Fun?

*Find a place inside where there's joy, and the joy will burn out the pain.*

—Joseph Campbell

"Relax! Have some fun!" We hear this all the time. Yet having fun is something that many of us don't know how to do effectively.

Let's examine what is having fun effectively. Frequent delving into hours of TV watching, or eating, or drinking is not effective, merely because it has consequences we are trying to avoid in first place: mental fatigue, weight accumulation, uncontrollable expressions of emotions. Buying expensive "toys," having extramarital love affairs, and generally escaping from self-control and direction isn't effective either. Sometimes we forget how to have fun and need direction and help.

Consumed by the daily routine, organization, and

over-scheduling to keep up with achieved success many of lack a tool-kit on what effective having fun actually is. The idea around having fun shows up prominently through connection with wisdom. The awakened ability to pay attention to enjoyment in life, awareness about their body and personal response system play transformative role for many seekers, leading them to a place of decisions around life satisfaction.

Kate was forty-four years old, tall, dark haired, and athletic. She looked and acted successful, a perfect example of a contemporary business-woman in her busy real estate practice. She stormed into my office, bringing in an air of business, schedules, and daily routine, slightly fatigues, pale yet with a professional sparkly smile. Upon our conversation she revealed that she works really hard to appear successful, because inside she feels empty. She was seeking spiritual guidance and clarity in her life purpose.

Spiritual work often begins as seeking purpose, particularly when for a while one has already experienced a sense of success and achievement in a certain area. Other areas need improvement, need to catch up with the ares of success, and it is not always obvious how to transfer the success from one area to the other.

When finally connected to her inner awareness, leading to guidance, in its core, it becomes obvious to Kate that the quality of life elevates when we have fun enjoying life. Often though, it is not clear that enjoyment means being in the moment and directing our attention to the sensations of pleasure of the moment.

This was Kate's second year of mentoring with me. Two years ago, she had been in a different place, asking questions like, "Why can't I have what I want?" She had matured and allowed herself a responsibility for her position in life. She now realized that in order to have something, she needed to give up something that stood in the way of her having what she wanted.

Initially I had explained that "why" questions put her in a passive position and caused her to experience life as if it was just happening to her. As soon as she turned to an active position and became the director of her life, she began to experience tremendous relief from pressures of having to defend her passive position and was now empowered by creative energy.

Previously, she had been living in an abusive relationship. Following wisdom from her spiritual wisdom, which directed her to have fun in her life, Kate created a boundary in her relationship and was able to really enjoy herself in a new quality in her relationship.

Two years later, Kate was focusing on the next step, looking to elevate her enjoyment.

In higher consciousness, she experienced her life on her own terms. I directed her to pay attention to her sensations in her experience of freedom while at work and then to notice what work she was doing when she experienced that sensation. She called it freedom when she was at liberty to decide the direction of her next action, giving her of a position of choice. She could decide what steps she needed to take to make it happen and be ready to commit to taking the decided action. Answers emerged easily pointing her to her life purpose and life fulfillment.

K: My purpose is to enjoy life. Have fun. Be the light. Shed the light to others.

In so many words, this was a restatement from two years ago. Then her life had been about finding fun in everything she encountered, just learning to have fun. As she accomplished that, her enjoyment needed refinement. Now it was about having fun in a refined way: being in the light. I led her to get a deeper experience of "shedding light." It is important that symbology is internally experienced at all angles. She replied by saying the following:

K: You know, being light filled and spilling the light

everywhere I go has to become my only way of being. People will see it. They will respond. They will smile, they will see my light, they will feel my light, and they will be reminded of their own light.

I asked her how she experienced the light, and she described it.

K: Have positive attitude, smile, and admire life. Have fun with life. No worries, no doubts, just playful fun. Like a child, carefree fun.

I asked her to experience herself having fun in her daily activities. The metaphor that represents light contains various behaviors on the plane of her reality. She began to enumerate the ways she shared the light in everyday occurrences and interactions in her work.

K: Do what I want to do only with light. Go where I want to go and bring light with me and remember to be on my path, keep my intention, walk with fun, do it all with fun, and be lively. Speak my thoughts clearly, easily. It feels easy to do it with light. I am seeing myself at work, speaking, showing, driving, negotiating, and having fun. I am amazed that it seemed stale to me before. Now it is all getting its sharpness again—clarity, precision.

I persisted, encouraging her to detail how she knew if something was fun. She responded by recognizing sensations in her body and describing them to me: an expanding horizontal swirl of energy around her chest, energy emanating throughout her body, energy rising from her pelvic area to her throat, her body overflowing with the excitement of being alive and feeling creative. When she experienced this, she indicated that nothing could disturb the field of knowing that emerged in her conscious awareness. The expanding energy overflowed the boundaries of her body, spilling over. She noticed tingling in her fingertips and toes, making her ready to explode in her inspired excitement of being alive. This was "having fun" for her.

The way she described her "having fun" sensation

was unique to her personal blueprint. It was her own idiosyncratic representation of who she was. For someone else it could be different, emerging from his or her own experience of the sensation. This was innate and just for her. All people have their own descriptions of how they are when they are most themselves. This is why it was important for Kate to have this experience in person. Experiencing this sensation, she shouted, "I want this!"

She asked how she could take this home and have this experience on her own. Her main guide, John, whose role was to guide her, invited her to go for a walk. He revealed to her, "You need to break out of the structure." She translated to me immediately, "I let the structure of the routine dictate the choices I make." The guide showed her the structure as a high castle, a shiny gold elongated structure built up high, representing the structure of beliefs imprinted on her since early childhood about her expectations of what a job is. She was locked in the castle tower.

Her other guide, Victor—a specialist in having fun—greeted her at the steps of this cathedral-like gateway. "Step outside with me."

K: He pulls me to step over the threshold. "Take a step," he says. And as I take a step, the ground suddenly gives, and I see him levitating above the ground. "You have to levitate like me," he says. I take a step, and suddenly I can levitate too! So we levitate together. It is fun!

She became aware of her sensations, describing in detail experiencing of expanding energy in her chest area, the feeling of lightness in her body. She noticed her usual sensation of heaviness was no longer present. The symbolism was clear: if she "levitates" through life, having fun, she will experience the feeling of fulfillment and satisfaction.

"Is it worth it for you?" I asked provocatively to see if she was motivated by this experience.

Her answer was linear.

K: If you don't levitate, you can't have it, can't have the satisfaction, fulfillment, all that you are craving. You can't have the work satisfaction that you want without this levitation. There is a swirl of energy that takes you, sweeps you, and it feels fun and exciting! They [guides] are constantly saying, "You are too serious. Have fun! The point is *not* where you are going or even what you are doing. It is to do it with fun, to have *fun*." Even the letters *F*, *U*, and *N* are waving side to side and up and down for me, having their own fun!

I asked her to get detail about ways to have fun on the job.

K: In regard to the job, they are saying, "You are working in a very stagnant way—old school, burying your head in your work. Wake up. Smell the proverbial coffee. Do more fun things. Be more fun!"

M: What does it mean to have more fun around the concept of your work?

K: "Work is fun when you do it with intention." That's what they say to me. Fun is to do what I want. "What's your intention?" they ask me.

M: When does the work become for you what you want? What work do you see yourself doing when you have fun?

K: He says he can't tell me what to do about my job, only that I need to have fun, be fun, live fun. But about the job, he can't tell. *I* have to decide that.

There was nothing surprising there, by the way. Even the most sophisticated of guides would never tell you to do or not do something you can decide on your own according to your free will. Kate would have to make a decision on her own, according to her free will, when she was ready. What they showed her was not to worry. Her decision would come to her when she was living with "fun."

# Fun and Life Satisfaction

As Kate's guides explore the fun with her, they will show her possibilities of directing her life. One of the three things will eventually happen. If she is experiencing fun, she can decide to approach her work from a perspective of something that pays bills so she can have fun outside of work, enjoying boat rides (she owned a boat) or gardening in her backyard. By holding a positive attitude and doing her best at her job, she can make the most fun in other areas of her life. The second choice is that she could change her job so she can have fun working in another position, company, or area of business. Finally—and this is the easiest—she could choose to approach her current work from a position of fun, with an attitude that this is the job that she wants to have. As a result, the level of enjoyment and life satisfaction would significantly change.

The guide invited her to step into the swirl the light and feel the energy. She was afraid. "I need to get prepared and levitate in that energy properly; otherwise, I will get swept by the swirl. I have to get a balancing stick and learn to balance myself."

The symbolic metaphor was very clear in this sentence. Before she stepped into her life in the new sense, she needed to approach it from the point of balance; otherwise, she would once again be swept away by distractions, shiny objects, new fads, and when she looked for having fun externally, she would lose control. Today, she is learning how to use her energy effectively and intentionally. Through guidance from her wisdom, who are now training her to differentiate, she is experiencing balanced fun again and again, over and over, and learning to create and recreate it before stepping into the swirl.

"The point is how you use energy," she kept repeating while doing the exercise her guide gave her. I was guiding her with questions to further deepen her awareness of herself having fun. The balancing stick was her metaphor for a position of balance when she was ready and impervious to the "swirls" of life. Because life will come up, if she isn't ready to take it on, she can't attend with intention to enhance her relationships, wealth, and health. Approached from a balanced position, having fun is easy.

# Wisdom VI: Exercise Your Body

*Leave all the afternoon for exercise and recreation,*
*which are as necessary as reading.*
*I will rather say more necessary because health is worth more*
*than learning.*

—Thomas Jefferson

## Exercise Your Body

*Commit to be fit.*

—Unknown

An instruction of the importance of physical exercise comes up regularly, to the surprise of both me and my clients. Nearly every session includes some strategies about how to integrate more physical movement, dance, and exercise into one's life and the importance of using one's body to raise levels of joy and flexibility. The guides offer insights into what develops when there is an increase of physical activity, whether it is athletic endeavors: biking, skiing, dancing or lovemaking. Almost always included are direct suggestions of deep breathing and physical movement with the subsequent motivating visualizations of improvement of quality of life.

Let's see how spiritual guidance points out some concrete benefits of exercising your body.

## Exercise for Weight Loss

I used to specialize in weight loss without diet. For some years I struggled with weight myself. So when I met Hannah, the topic was familiar. My work with Hannah at her request was devoted to her self-perception. She felt she was overweight and wanted to return to her "normal" size. She was healthy, and over the last few months, as the pressures of her job increased, she had tried dieting but gained the weight back each time. Hannah was tall enough to be able to carry her extra weight gracefully, but she was concerned with her image, the way clothes fit her, and her health. I noticed that she moved in a tentative way, displaying an inability to control her movements, which usually shows up in those who spend a lot of their time sitting at their desks and not using their musculature for support.

At thirty-nine, Hannah remarked that her scheduling was tight and disallowed physical activity. She continued to spend more and more time at her desk and often snacked to elevate her energy. Her decreasing self-esteem made her job difficult; she often found herself seeking approval from others and asking for feedback on her appearance. She was unsure of what she needed to do, whether lose weight or color her hair, so she could gain self-confidence.

Hannah had been on a spiritual path for many years. In her youth, she had meditated. Over the years, she had lost the connection with her spiritual side, but she remained very interested in her role in the universe. Entering into a wisdom state, she connected with her guides, and they spoke to her, and she relayed it to me.

H: You are very powerful, they convey. You are magical, so what is in you and what goes into you must be magical too. Thoughts you think must be pure. Food that you eat must be magical. Prepare your food with love. That makes it tasty and magical. Live your life with magic. Then magic happens on the outside of you.

This seemed to impact her, and she paused. Then she continued.

H: Humans are spiritual beings, yet we influence each other through our bodies because the way we experience ourselves is through our physical representations—our bodies. In a spiritual sense, we "choose" our bodies carefully. I have a lovely, gorgeous body that suits my purpose; it's easy for me to attract attention when I make a point because I am tall and dominant. Yet I am not beautiful. People are beautiful when they are healthy in body and in spirit. Those who are healthy look beautiful. They don't have to be beautiful; their energy makes them attractive! They are confident, and they carry a message. Then other people listen to those who have healthy, beautiful energy, which is attractive to the message they carry. I have low, sad energy because I am unsure of my message to people. Oh, now I get it! It is a symbiotic relationship between the body and the message I carry in me, of my purpose here, of my intention, of my passion. How do I make my energy attractive? I have to take care of myself and my physical body.

She paused again to process what was being revealed to her. I let her have her time.

H: When I was just a soul without a body before coming to this life, I considered another body of a handsome man from India. He carried arrogant energy because of his narcissistic beauty, and I chose the body of a woman who was not so self-oriented. I had a past life as a woman living in a rural Poland in the 1800s. She was beautiful yet did not appreciate herself. She depleted her own energy by locking herself in the house after her fiancée did not return from the war. She was sitting by the window, sewing all day long, year after year. That life was dull and unproductive. I got another chance in my beauty to awaken my inner energy. In my feminine body, energy is flowing up from my root into my heart. A beautiful flower unfolds at my pelvis as I breathe in, sending energy to my chest, and in my heart I am connected with my soul center. There I am *Aiyah*.

The sound of that name was sung to her rather than spoken: a convergence of melodic intonations that created a mood into which one could be immersed. This is not unusual in these guidance revelations. She sang the name to me, relaying the beauty of the tone.

H: When the energy flows into my heart, I come awake. Right now the flow is stopped halfway, at the level of my navel, because I feel weak in my feminine power.

I asked her guide to show her the exercise she could use to empower herself.

H: I am offered to focus on the light. Center myself in the body of light. Just position myself inside the strong bright light. See and feel the colors, a variety of colors, which have different frequencies with different healing properties. Pink is for love. Innocence is gold. Higher light, which interacts with Earth energies, is blue, and it is cool and restoring. Green is also healing but mostly for a human body, cooling the aches. Earthy tones like beige and brown work with different colors, dimming some unnecessary interference. Sometimes that is necessary to make them more powerful in smaller doses.

I asked who directed the light to be a particular color and who determined which color was needed for her, particularly for her self-esteem.

H: I determine that as I set my intention for healing, letting go, empowerment, self-knowledge, love, or connection. The color you need appears; it is given to you. Once you get to know what color enhances your energy, you can use that color more often. You can wear those colors more often. You can wear gemstones like lapis, which is blue for communication. Rose quartz is for setting my intention on love. Yellow topaz is for self-expression; wear it on your throat or heart or solar plexus and enjoy free expression. Music produces frequencies as colors do. Sound produces light. Complimentary light vibrations cancel sickness vibrations. Pour music into your body to take care of yourself. Music is just a way of living your life. Music is rhythm, pulse, vibration, light.

I asked her to tell me about her own rhythm.

She attuned to the inner information in her body, receiving signals of her own rhythm. She listened and naturally moved, swaying and tapping her foot every other sway, as if listening to a musical tune in her head, or rather in her body.

H: My rhythm is natural, and it is red. Red color brings up good emotions, safety, security, like the first blanket I had as a child. It feels good to experience the rhythm. Moving in this rhythm is like being in a cradle—safe, comfortable. There is a tune I don't know, but I can probably sing the tune now.

She sang a soft continuous tune, highlighting the rhythm.

H: My song is not written yet. It is for me to write. I must do it to feel good. And I must feel good to write it. Write my own song.

Her guides' directive was to stay positive, sleep well, exercise, and eat good, natural, and fresh food—food that grew in the light.

H: My body responds when I take care of myself, and I can feel it in my expression. I feel the clarity in my body's expression of itself. It is a bit awkward at first. But I like it. It is exciting. They add, "Exercise your body, go biking, walk, do yoga, dance. All you need to do is yoga for the mind and the body together. Exercise your body so it remains agile, flexible, and disease free. This is to align the higher energy of the place and your energy.

This is the easiest thing to do to keep the alignment. Keep yourself aligned. Let yourself feel pure joy, harmony, and sound. Make good choices, relax your body, make yourself loose and flexible, and exercise so you can control your movement. It feels good, and it makes you confident in your body. When you are confident in your body, you are confident in your mind. Relax, ease your mind, and feel in your heart love and peace. It is easy to stay in balance like that, like a ballerina on a point of her foot. Feel the balance, not trying to control it but riding it with the natural rhythm of your body. Connect to your rhythm. Keep your head up. Breathe deeply. Smile. Feel the wellness in your body. Positive, centered in your core."

I directed her to describe the details of her experiencing the wellness in her body so that she could later know how to recreate that sensation by creating the physical experience of it. There was a long pause during which she moved to realign herself several times, slowly with very small incremental motions, and settled in to a more balanced position.

H: Wow … I feel it now … Easier with each time. It feels so right, better and more deeply detailed.

Hannah described more details of her posture, with her core upright, and slightly moved forward as if she was ready to stand up to go do something else and take the next action. As she sat like that, her face was alight with internal excitement; her eyebrows were raised as if her eyes were wide open, yet they were closed; and she was experiencing all that detailed diversity of the experience inside herself. Then she suddenly turned her head toward me and said, "I just let go of my past."

She explained that while she was sitting in that "ready" position, listening to her rhythm, she was reminded about her ex-boyfriend, and positioned like that she could not connect to her long-term grudge toward him, could not feel the usual tension she experienced when thinking of him. Hannah was amazed. Just like that, she released him, and she felt ready to go onto the next stage of her life open to a new relationship.

H: It is important for me to remember this feeling. It is a tingling, prickly feeling in my lower abdomen. It is excitement, and it gives me confidence. It is important to remember to feel centered, grounded and start from there.

She continued with the wisdom from her guide.

M: It's time to let go of fake seriousness. It is time to be myself and laugh and have fun. Simple joy of connection. Even if I think it is really hard, it is not so hard. It is easier than I ever thought. I feel so connected now. My companions are all here, led by my grandmother, to remind me to stay centered. She comes to remind me of being in the light in the face of challenge, to stay loving and joyful.

Hannah's grandmother showed her the way to balance herself.

H: First you have to relax, center yourself, and move your body into a symmetrical position in space. Support yourself by your own strength in your core, not melting or sliding but elongating yourself upward and forward toward the source—which is above and ahead of you—and downward through the root toward the center of the Earth. Inner core stretches to strengthen and support you.

Again Hannah sat up.

H: I feel that! Secondly, you have to connect. Check your energy centers to be aligned—your root, your heart, and your crown. Send the energy from your root upward through your heart and your crown and outward toward the source. Find that the alignment is complete with your mind aware of your body and its surroundings and at the same time aware of the connection with the source and your intention. Then the energy from your core will reach your chest, your heart will open, and the spark of light will come out forward to illuminate your path.

She sat like this for a while and then spoke again.

M: It says if I want to move forward with my intention, now is the time.

## Exercise for Desired Pregnancy

Lizzy's guidance gave clear instructions and made clear to her the importance of physical preparation of her body and her mind for the next round of conception. Lizzy was an entertainer and successful in everything except motherhood. She had been shooting her new video program under the pressure of a deadline when she was rushed to the hospital with a miscarriage. At thirty-eight, she came to me distressed, seeking guidance on how to nurture and regenerate herself, bounce back to create a new life, and take spiritual steps to create physical life.

I asked if she often fantasized about having a baby. She responded by shaking her head. "No, that's too far ahead! I have to first make my body conceive. We've been trying for a few years, but I am just too busy to think about what comes after."

Her guides were very direct in pointing out wisdoms to her, as there was no time to be wasted. She needed to change her attitude and toward her own body first. She needed to live the magic of her body first and not use it as a machine. She needed to change her attitude toward her relationship and not use it as a machine for conception or the fulfillment of her expectations. And surely she needed to change her attitude toward her baby. If the baby were to come to her, she had to make time to attend to her body, her life, and her love.

L: Breathe. Live each day as if it is your last day. I am told to breathe deeply and slowly. Love yourself. Give yourself what you need: air, fresh food, love, nurturing. Exercise your physical core. You can't contribute anything if you are unhealthy and depleted. Your energy is contaminated with bad thinking and sadness. Get rid of that. Get rid of time. There is no time. All comes in time. Keep your energy going strong. You must exercise your body three to four times a week to remain youthful, strong, and free from illness.

Knowing how busy she was in her week, I asked for her commitment.

M: Well, are you ready to do this? How can you schedule this into your week?

She responded quickly.

L: It's all worked out already. I'll get up at 5:30 a.m. and exercise before work. It is easy for me.

I insisted.

M: Will you do it?

L: I already feel being in shape just seeing myself do it! I feel I am already getting more confident just seeing myself exercising. Besides, it is easier to manage stress and have a great day. I am already doing it! I am wearing shorts and a baseball hat and go running on the beach with my dog. My thighs look good, no flab. I feel great! I am having a great day! I can manage anything that comes my way. My husband is happier. I can see it. We have a better relationship. We have time for each other because I have more energy.

I was curious about what came next. She continued.

L: Then in time I have a healthy pregnancy, and the baby comes maybe even the same time next year.

Lizzy conceived shortly after our start of work together. We continued to work together, and she had a healthy baby. She was able to work it out so that she had more time for being a mom, and she loves it. We continue to revisit her guidance for updates on her intentions and commitments as she goes on.

# Wisdom VII: Create Intention

*One way or another, we all have to find what best fosters the flowering of our humanity in this contemporary life, and dedicate ourselves to that.*

—Joseph Campbell

## What's Intention?

*Our intention creates our reality.*

—Wayne Dyer

My journeyers know my interests are quite eclectic. I like to attend intellectually stimulating discussion clubs, book reviews, meet ups with iconic topics like Jungian archetypes, and neuroscientific presentations. Last spring I was invited by a scientist friend to a lecture at Cooper Union. The speaker was one of my favorite neuroscientists, Michael Gazzaniga. His topic was "*Who's In Charge? Free Will and the Science of the Brain,*" which is also a title of his latest book on the subject.

Who is actually in charge in our lives? Who makes decisions? Is it our bodies, our minds, or our brains, or do we really have free will to make decisions?

I find this topic provocative. Many claim that they are in charge, yet Gazzaniga humorously states that what we understand as free will is only a *current* intention we have, not the long term one: *"The brain has millions of local processors making important decisions...There is no one boss in the brain. You are certainly not the boss of the brain. Have you ever succeeded in telling your brain to shut up already and go to sleep?"*

Kidding aside, our habitual behavior combined with an array of our neurophysiology of reflexes, leads us to move toward "pleasure" and away from "discomfort" almost automatically. Coming from an overpowering family with two "helicopter parents," and a background of strong views, powerful fear tactics, and frequent interruptions, I appreciate the point that a "moving away" strategy can also be a powerful driver.

One can find themselves moving away from something they dislike and create a powerful drive for themselves to action. However, just moving away is not enough to go in a particular singular direction, toward achieving a determined outcome.

For example, constantly moving away from pain, does not create health. Constantly moving away from weight issues, personal insecurities, or poverty does not in itself create desired self-perception, perfect figure, or wealth. Even having a single desired outcome, like to have a relationship, a result, that is tangible, does not help us move in that direction other than moving away from being single.

Back in my "heavy" times, I tried dieting many times for many reasons. I wanted to run away from disease and be more attractive so I didn't remain single. That was a survival tactic. After the dieting was over, the weight usually came back. At the time, I had no idea that I had to make a lifestyle change, eat healthier on a consistent basis, and exercise to burn calories and generate energy. It is only when I have eliminated diet, and make a healthy lifestyle a norm I began to see changes in my body in the direction I desired.

So just moving away is not enough.

Moving toward is an active action that is an essential ingredient to achieving a goal.

However, many of us know surprisingly little about what to do to create that movement, and mostly because knowing about our direction is vague, unclear and uncertain.

Creating clarity around our future, determining the results with clarity and then backtracking to the path we took to achieve that is a very effective method in manifesting results.

We all want something in our lives. Previous success in one area may be indicative of a natural talent or a trained skill, proclivity and persistence. Then we can translate the understanding of how one outcome is created into another area and make it a part of our long-term direction. In order for the success to be manifest, all other directions must be pruned. Keeping focus on intention helps create consistent results and strengthens success. Even though moving away from discomfort can be a powerful driver, having an intention defines a direction in which it is easier to move forward and toward something that is desirable rather than just away from what is not desirable.

## How Can We Create Clarity in Our Intention?

*Clarity affords focus.*

-Kafka

Recent brain science discoveries about spiritual hypnotic journeys suggest that long term changes take place in our brains during interactive experience of spiritual awareness. As self-discovery revelations take place, certain areas of the brain are activated creating new neural pathways for firing the signals to the areas of decision making and action. When decisions are made regarding important life-changing commitments, emotional connections positively affect our physical ability to project into our future, we experience the future at present as if it is happening now resulting in growing ability to follow the chosen path.

The decisions that are made in a state of discovery are profound and long lasting and are amplified through emotional connection with the result elevating awareness. The awareness of the future now positively alters their ability to create and modify their futures in the way they desire.

## Is It Possible to Predict the Future?

*The empire of the future is the empire of the mind.*

-Winston Churchill

This provocative question has entertained humanity for many generations. The process that I utilize in spiritual awareness through gamma hypnosis emphasizes the client's ability to look into the future and predict the events with desired precision. Yet, predicting does not mean that we don't have to do anything to get to that predicted point.

Many people seem to have a desire to have control over their futures. Imagine you can see into your future. Would you be willing to accept it? How would you be willing to change now to ensure that the future is more to your liking?

This is exactly what spiritual guides suggest: if you are not getting what you want, change now so you can have what you want.

But why change? What is the motivational driver to

transformation? If things remain the way they are, could we have what we want?

From my experience with the results my clients have, it seems that in a state of higher consciousness clients' experiences of connecting with internal information related to intention produces concrete images of the future. Images, sensations, sounds, and experiences are immediately translated into a narrative based on their subconscious symbolic representations and personal beliefs.

Throughout thousands of years of world mythology as explored by Joseph Campbell and others, the concept of being able to predict the future on the basis of unexplained creative interpretation was revered. Those who were able to look into the future (shamans, healers, witches, oracles, gurus, and psychics) were and are feared and revered.

Yet the suggestion is that the ability to look into the future is available to all of us. We all can and have a responsibility to ourselves to be the people to look into our own futures and construct in imagination the futures we want, thus creating trajectories for our own futures. This must be done in an ongoing way, not just on occasion.

As part of the preparation to a spiritual experience, an individual must become aware of his or her intention and responsibility for the receiving the information he or she requests. The interaction with his or her spiritual guidance is determined by what he or she believes he or she will do with the information at the end of the encounter.

Believe it or not, many people are not committed to taking action based on the information they receive. The familiarity with their current discomfort overrides their perceived anticipation of the discomfort they imagine may come with change. In the past, their commitments may have faulted, or the effort to achieve did not pay off.

The familiar saying that best describes this type

of resistance is, "The devil you know is better that the devil you don't know." This malevolent attitude and the prevalent stigma attached with making a misstep locks many people into holding on to patterns of disappointment, sadness, and disease.

Even though the adventure may bring them real satisfaction and fulfillment, uncertainty and fear prevents them from going on the journey. They begin to anticipate the failure of trying. This is a "refusal of the call to adventure."

## How Intention Works

*Our intention creates reality.*

-Wayne Dyer

Once our intention for the future outcome is set, we begin to focus our attention to seek out the necessary experiences relating to our intentions. We seek the signals in the environment that designate the direction toward that outcome.

For example, if you are set to resolve relationship patterns and learn what could be helpful to do so in order to have the relationship of your dreams, you set that as intention. A large portion of your experience then becomes organized to make manifest that intention: the relationship of your dreams.

The trajectory from the present to the future begins to change, having absorbed the knowledge of what future came to your conscious awareness. The present experience begins to accommodate for the changing trajectory of the movement into the intended future, therefore changing the future outcomes. Even though intended previously, as new unknown forms of those outcomes emerge, the future changes. After one change occurs, a piece of knowledge is added to the system, and the next sequence is modified. This is called updating the system based on feedback resulting from actions taken toward a particular outcome.

Take a peek at the brilliant metaphor in the movie *Back to the Future* with Michael J. Fox. When Mr. Fox's character finds himself in the past with his parents before they were married and the opportunity arises for him to make changes by being there, he takes the challenge to make sure that the future he creates by being in the past is the way he wants it upon his return. He must make sure that whatever he does in that past strengthens his position in the future, not jeopardizes it.

My clients really enjoy learning from their projections into the future, when they will have accomplished what they wanted. From there, they retrace the steps that led to that success and eliminate any obstacles by playing future scenarios using the success skills and strategies of their past experiences (or past lives) and making informed decisions to take the next step in their current situations.

I teach them to ask their guides the necessary questions in order to know what happened to make that happen.

Often, according to your set intention, the information becomes available with a certain degree of precision and clarity, and any change in the desired direction becomes possible.

In my opinion, everyone can experience looking into their futures by setting their intentions at least into the nearest future, two to three weeks or two to three months at a time. Then they become emotionally involved with this future, with an opportunity to choose it. That determines their level of commitment and subsequent actions toward it. Deciding to amend actions as they bring results, they create their futures to be how they want. The future becomes predictable, exciting, and yet magical.

Let's examine a few positive benefits of intention.

## Intention for Balance

Lisa, thirty-four, was a creative performer. Her creativity allowed her to see beauty in everything, and she expressed herself easily with movement, dance, and teaching creative movement to an exclusive list of clients. Yet she sought a deeper expression in her creativity. She wanted to enhance her career with a complimentary self-expression. But what direction to pick? Open a school, add more students, or teach another creative subject? Her guides encouraged her to balance her intense emotions about each question, urging her to listen to her sensations in a balanced way. Her guides showed her the importance of setting and adhering to an intention that defined her outcome. She was guided to pay attention to what the intention brought and how it felt. The guides offered an intense training in self-assessment of her own sensation, which was needed to determine what intention was the right one. Her guides were training her to experience her inner wisdom in its fullness and determine ways to balance and life experience.

L: You are always living in your intention but not always aware of the being in balance. Once you are always aware of your balance, whatever your life's intention is becomes clear. It is a feeling. Is the feeling of doing it the right one for you? Then go ahead. Bring this spirit in and have an experience of your life. Only then can you have what you want.

## Intention for Life Fulfillment

A university professor, Eric, was in his sixties and was seeking meaning to, as he called it, his second half of life. He wanted to know his next step toward completing the fulfillment of his purpose. Working with his guides, he was shown the intention in being as a main way to complete the fulfillment of purpose.

Eric experienced himself in a wonderful state of

fulfillment in which he needed nothing, and his only wish was to continue to know more about this relaxing and fulfilling state of his being. He became aware of his intention, purpose, and ways to behave so that he could bring this fulfillment with him to physical existence. He perceived himself as light, and as he described the details of that perception to me, I led him to place his focus on finding answers to questions he posed.

E: There is bright light ahead. There is bright light around me. I ask, "Who am I?" The answer is that I am light. I cannot see. I feel the light being inside me, inspiring me, energizing me. I also experience that there is no separation, no difference between me and any other person. It means to me that our lights overlap. We interact even though we don't know it. Our energies mix.

M: What is true of you?

E: My true nature is space and light. I experience myself being aware, more awake, filled with knowledge as light illuminates my body, and I do have a body that is physical and that I can control it by directing my awareness to it.

M: What is your purpose?

E: My purpose is to know myself and know there is no separation with the other. I am part of everything and everyone else. I have to be very careful what I eat, where I place my attention, and what my direction is because the rest of the world depends on my mindful behavior. So I have to be very intent in it.

M: Determine your intention.

E: My intention is to live a purposeful life, fulfill my purpose to love, live beyond the limitations of mind, and in love learn to let go. Love cannot control. Love gives, generously and beyond limitation. I need to explore the depth of my mind, mature, not place so much importance on things, events, and people that are limiting, not attach myself to things or physical forms, just be the essence of mind. Suffering comes from lack of discipline and stupidity in paying attention to obstacles instead of the road itself.

M: What is your journey?

E: Part of my journey is to find the true nature of myself.

M: How do you get to know your true nature?

E: Spend more time with me, get to know me, be close to nature, and stop fear because it is lack of emotional maturity. Learn to meditate, learn to love, and learn patience so I can give others what they need of me.

M: How do you know what they need of you and what to give?

E: I can learn love, and love is generous. It is also evolving people who give and who receive. True love is light.

## *Intention to Do What You Love*

A professional business coach, Nina leads people to their success. We worked together a few years ago, and after that Nina created a flourishing center for those who seek personal advancement. She calls this finding her purpose. Nina felt the need to deepen her awareness of her own success patterns to make her even more effective.

M: What is the purpose of you being here in this life?

N: I am here to learn to be myself. Being myself is easy. When I am by myself, I am myself, totally. It's not much different from how I have always been—light and funny, creative and bouncing back to life if I stumble. I see the way to make my contribution to other people's life experiences by being with them in the way I am most myself. Does it make sense? To me it makes a lot of sense.

M: How are you when you are yourself?

N: Wow, I am a free spirit, a breeze, a light that moves.

I am rhythm and movement. I am clarity and focus. I am action and stillness all at the same time.

She smiled and became silent for a while. I felt it was an emotional moment for her and gave her space to experience it to the fullest. In a while, I saw her emotion; a small tear ran out of the corner of her eye and down her cheek. I continued to be silent.

N: I am so touched. I am so honored, so privileged to be the light. I am here to be the light. To shine light. There is nothing else, just be the light. It is *being* the light. Then the light shines outwardly.

She went silent. I waited for a few moments. Then she spoke again.

N: I am just experiencing being the light. I am simultaneously the source of light and all creation and the catalyst through which the light from the source passes and becomes light, more light. Like this I shine, I can ... shine. It means a lot to me, to be light for others.

M: What can you do like this, being the light?

N: I can do anything. Nothing is impossible.

M: Can you be like this with your clients?

N: I know exactly what to do to lead others to their better lives. It means I have to live my life as an example of a life in which I do the best I can. That's a big step for me. I have to always do my best and keep in mind that I am living my life to the top. Be the oasis so others can drink from my well ... It is relieving in a way to know that I can do something this concrete and also so freeing. I am not restricted to just doing what I am expected to do. That's boring. I want that. Not only may I, but I have to do what I want. Well, I can see it now. I am doing the best I can. I couldn't know to do any better ... The best foot forward, with the best intention, keeping in mind the purpose of my doing it.

M: Doing what?

N: Everything! Eating, sleeping, and other stuff. It all has a purpose. No, not *it has. I do*. I do everything with a purpose. With intention. I am doing the best I can in getting enough sleep. It is good already. What is it I can do even better? Like putting my focus to the project and giving it all I can. Not halfway if it might work out or others will pick it up. All the way. Feel the feeling now of all the way. Commit to life all the way. Love all the way. Live all the way. Wow, I don't even know what that's like! Now I can feel it. They are showing me the feeling! Oh my God! That's awesome. Why would I do it any other way? I wouldn't do it any other way!

## Intention for Making a Difference

Sheila was looking to create a legacy, to make a difference, and to help her community. She had the means to contribute but was not aware of what she could do. Guides told her she was coming from the wrong place. She needed to create an intention and live it. Guides gave Sheila direct advice. They spoke to her in second person, addressing her in conversation, and she relayed it to me.

S: You are very special. You are here to touch lives. You have intuition. Listen to it. Meditate. Don't be afraid.

M: What is their advice?

S: The structure needs to change. Not conducive in the corporate place where you are. You cannot be part of something of which the focus and purpose is different than yours.

Sheila's philosophy was not the same as the philosophy of the place where she worked. She needed to change the place of her energy focus and look for another way to apply herself.

S: Focus on making the difference in other people's lives. You need to start working with people in a different way and seek good people who support what you do, your ideas, what you believe, and most importantly who you are.

M: What is the next step?

S: You need to re-examine your rules, your beliefs. Start with balance. Start your work today. Don't wait. Connect each morning. Create your day. Create your life.

M: How do you start that work?

S: Don't think of this as work. Work is just what you do toward the result. What result do you want? Set your intention.

## Intention for the Right Thing

Erin, thirty-nine, was looking to figure out a solution for her family situation. She wanted to conceive a baby, and her larger family was attaching a lot of meaning to it, yet in the last seven years, she and her husband had been unsuccessful and even tried artificial insemination. Erin was a successful fashion designer and worked endless hours on her patterns. Yet it never occurred to her to use her vivid imagination to create her family in her head first as she did with her designs.

M: What is your guidance advising?

E: I have to stop drama; it is just irritation. Breathe air, freedom, beauty, joy, peace, feel happy to be myself. Who am I? I am a girl in a thin dress with rope tied around my waist, looking at a water pond, flowers around, waterfall behind. I bring love wherever I go. I forgot my purpose. Now I remember. I allowed drama to take over. I have to go back and do the right thing.

M: What's the right thing?

E: Love who I am and give myself to others. Let others love me. Let my husband love me. When you are yourself, it is easy to love you.

Erin's husband had made some personal and financial mistakes, and she had been hard on herself and him. She had kept anger deep in her abdomen. Guides saw everything and advised her to let go.

E: Forgive those who make mistakes. Believe in

yourself. Be strong. Enjoy your life. Be happy. You are scared, and happiness slips away. Stop the fear. Be brave, solid, calm, and breathe. Meditate. Start exercising. Don't wait. Start now. Be patient. Be respectful to yourself first. Be kind. Be sensitive to others. Fulfill yourself. Learn to feel better in your physical body. Exercise. Enjoy your body. Love yourself.

## Intention for Creativity

Rina was a creative director for a major TV studio. She was in her late forties and wanted to learn how to make meaning in her life and how to be in order to attract a loving relationship, a companion.

Her guide came with unusual advice: the intention would become be clear when she was at her best. Then the intention was the only road to take.

R: No one is holding me back from achieving my goals. My intention is to bring the best out first in myself and then in others, to help them, to guide them, to point them in the right direction. To help them identify what talents they have and help them use their talents. To provide solace. I am a part of creative force in the universe. I am here to experience what the creative force in the universe can do, learn to isolate fear, learn to love in harsh environments, learn to trust and love those who cannot love me back, love myself more, and be kind and peaceful.

M: How will you need to do it?

R: Communicate through writing, speaking, and sharing the knowledge about the meaning of life. By helping serve others, they are empowered to overcome obstacles and to be the best they can be. I can help them fulfill their purpose.

M: And then what?

R: Then I am fulfilled. Believe in myself, trust, be confident, and don't let others' issues get in the way of progress. Motivate others and help them be more confident by being myself, happy.

M: How can you become happy?

R: Only I can make myself happy. No one else can make me anything. Happiness ... you see, everyone wants it, and yet they think someone out there needs to come and hand it to them. I was one of those. Stop procrastinating. Stop depending on others for approval. They don't have the right to approve or disapprove of you, only you do. Believe in yourself. Have fun living.

M: What is your purpose?

R: My purpose is love, laughter, and simplicity. They make the world happier. I make laughter, write funny stories, be funny, be fun. Laughter is part of a happy life. Compassion captures the essence of true love.

Rina was looking to make a choice between the two men she was dating. I asked her to get guidance on that.

R: If I am me, I will do the right thing. I will make the right choice. The right choice for all concerned. They say, "You will know the right choice." It has love in it. Choose one direction and have my energy in one place.

Sometimes we don't realize how important it is to find guidance in questions like this. Once you are the way you want to be, it is easy to make the right choice. Of course, she was able to choose.

## Intention for Action

Lane was a marketing consultant. He divided his time between a broken home with three kids and his busy work. Lane was forty-four and was looking to make meaning in his life, which seemed a constant busy pattern of running from one task to the next and making hasty decisions and compromises. I only asked questions, and his guide—a tall angelic woman—brought answers filled with wisdom. The guide was called Rachel, and she called Lane out on his internal conflict.

M: What is your purpose?

L: Stop lying. Stop pretending. Be yourself. Just be yourself.

M: How will you need to be to be yourself?

L: I need to learn to overcome my inner complacence, to do 100 percent. Don't give up. There can be a different ending.

M: What do you need to do to meet your soul mate?

L: She will be my mate if circumstances are met.

M: What circumstances?

L: "If you didn't give up," she says, "you would have met me already." She also adds, "You don't need anybody's help. Take responsibility for what you need to do and just do it." And then she says, "Stop lying!"

M: Are you lying?

L: Yes, I am. I am not honest with myself. I am trying to make things fit.

M: What things?

L: My work. I am not honest. I do it just for money. I should be doing more creative work. I know what I should be doing. But I need time and money to do it. I am too overwhelmed. My mind is lazy. I am putting things off.

He paused and smiled peacefully.

L: But she says, "Cut the crap. Get a grip on yourself." She loves me.

M: Did she really say, "Cut the crap"?

L: Yes, that's her language. She can be very authoritative. I have never seen her this way before though. She says I don't have too much to time to be lazy here. She said, "Don't forget how strong you are."

M: How can you apply your strength?

L: Feel good instead of being terrified. It takes strength, mental strength. She advises me to love myself, go to nature, get energy, recharge, plug in to get reenergized, stop interrupting myself, and ... stop lying! It will make a difference. I am on the right path. I must keep listening to my heart, not to my ego, and my life will change. I can do it. I can welcome anything I want.

He was silent for a while and then spoke again.

L: Her name is Rachel. She brings opportunity, implementing change, but there will be consequences. I know it. My life will change. Part of why I was putting this off was that I could see the consequences. I can't go on with the compromise anymore. It is like playing with fire.

He contemplated. Then as if he made a decision, he sat up.

L: She says, "Otherwise, whose life are you living? There are other ways. Courage to take the unknown path. The sooner you live life in this way, the greater the chances are that we will meet and you will be happy." It feels happy! She says I can always bring her back to my mind for encouragement. Powerful … My mind is powerful. I need to use it to make my life what I want.

## Intention for Finding Meaning

Laura was a scientist and was focused on doing her research project. She wanted to know more about the ways to go about the project for its success.

L: It is important to show the different stages of it and describe it in each step. I don't have to go to the end of the way, this other guy's way; his hypothesis is wrong. If we gather more information, we'll make a difference. All we need is to change the angle as we look at it so that it becomes the flow. I can see both the big picture and small details at the same time. It's awesome to capture the whole and zoom into parts of it. Concentrated and generalized. I am sifting the information. I am a figure inside the sand clock, an hourglass; I am inside the glass as the information comes through me. I have in my house a blue sand clock like this. I am in the middle, writing in a sacred book with golden pages. A ray of light is writing through me, and I give it substance by holding it. I hear the words; it is writing through me.

M: What's the essence of the writing?

She gave me a long scientific tirade. I wrote it down. Now what, I asked her.

L: The horizon lights up in the air near me, lights near me, in a distance. So many lights. The air is made from particles of light. The earth is made up from particles of light. I am light. You are light. We are all one light. My guides came, twelve of them. They are dressed as clowns.

M: Really? Why is that?

L: They say it's a party. It's always a party to see me. They have all the vibrant colors on, triangle hats. Ha-ha! They have a warm and loving energy. I am asking them what I am here for, and they show me a boat. They are showing me that the boat is sealed and can't sink. At the same time, it has no borders, like it's impenetrable. Defined shape but flexible boundaries. A very curious device.

M: What is it for? How does it work?

I couldn't ask her for the meaning because this question would involve conscious thinking. As a scientist, she was very literal, so from her wisdom guidance, I gently led her to ask them to explain how it worked so we could later we discuss the meaning of this metaphorical symbol.

L: Oh, that's for my emotional protection. I need to be daring. So the boundaries are flexible. We are flexible. There needs to be flexibility. The energy is moving through it up-down, down-up, sideways, as it is translucent, infinitely connected. Diamond sparkling rays in all directions penetrate it, giving it meaning. This is our energy. This is life.

M: What's the purpose of life?

L: Life just is. The purpose of life is life itself. Living

life is the purpose. Enjoy living life and you will find satisfaction. That's how it is.

I was amazed how wise in its simplicity the guidance from higher awareness was and how easy life seemed if we only followed this guidance.

# Wisdom VIII: Stay in the Light

*You don't have a soul. You are a Soul. And you have a body.*

—C.S. Lewis

## Light

*To love beauty is to see light.*

—Victor Hugo

### Light and Dark

Appreciation of beauty is a skill. There are people who can see beauty in everything. We call that carrying the light. Light is beautiful.

Finding beauty in life is a skill. Just like training the mind to think positive thoughts instead of indulging in dark and depressive ones, finding light in everything you experience is a trained skill, and it takes practice.

Why would you want it? Simply, so you can enjoy your life to the fullest. Let me explain.

What does it mean to stay in the light?

When I started to work with accessing higher wisdom

through spiritual regression, I realized I had to make a choice: the choice between dark and light.

I decided to choose the light. The difference between dark and light is very simple. Everything that is less than pure light is dark. Dark is not light, and light is not dark. I associate darkness with fear, and sensations of moving away, avoidance. I associate light with joy. Light creates a sensation of desire to move toward what creates that sensation.

Fear is dark. Fear is a very strong emotion, and it is created by doubt. The moment doubt sets in one little question or area, all other areas are immediately affected. People who live in the dark or spend a lot of time in the dark tend to find faults, blame others, and find things to complain and grumble about.

People who spend time in the dark often display their dark tendencies by criticizing others without offering constructive alternatives. They indulge in browbeating without seeking active solutions. They tell people, "This is not what I had in mind," without telling what they did have in mind or wanted instead. They live their lives using a "moving away" strategy. You certainly know such people; they tend to speak about what they want using descriptions of what they don't want or don't like or are afraid of.

They tend to live in fear of something they don't want to happen, holding onto the past, holding grudges, saving their best shot as a "last resort." They stand alone, move aside, often gossip, and ask rhetorical questions like, "Why me?" Dark people rarely enjoy themselves or people around them, their jobs, or anything that happens in their lives. They often think they are missing out on something, envy others, and feel angry at others because they have something good. Dark people are not proud of the team they may be working with; in fact, they try to diminish others' achievements in favor of themselves. Often it's not that the dark person wants something; it's that he or she doesn't want others to have what he or she can't.

On the other end of the spectrum are people who live in the light. You know such people; they light up from the inside. They have resiliency and are upbeat whatever happens; they let go, and they tend to smile a lot and look on the brighter side of things. Most of the time light people are also aesthetically pleasing and possess some degree of inner and outer beauty and congruency in their image.

They move a project along by offering solutions. If they work in a team, they identify themselves as team members and acknowledge that each person has his or her own strengths and weaknesses. Light people emphasize others' positive qualities, strengths, and "sweet spots" to move the project along.

As team players, they think in terms of how to get things done in the most effective way for the benefit of the team. They are open to suggestions and don't take criticism personally. They try to do their best and speak thoughtfully. Light people find positive patterns of success and capitalize on what works. They point out what really works and what is positive and in line with intention. They admit if others do things better than them and are not afraid to speak their minds. As managers, light people give the team a mandate and then stand out of the way to let the team accomplish the goal instead of checking and micromanaging.

So what's it like to be in the light? Let's hear it from people experiencing the light.

## Stay in the Light for Confidence

Sonya was a new partner at a large law firm. She was only thirty-three and felt under pressure to "perform," or in her words, "to prove herself worthy" of the new position. She was looking for confidence. Her higher guidance led her to experience herself in her future as confident. She described it as "light." I asked her to elaborate on this description in order to make this experience memorable for her and to inspire her curiosity to gain clarity on what it meant to be confident for herself.

S: I see myself in the future, fearless. How did I become so fearless? I want to ask this, but I don't need to ask. I already know. I just feel the light, and that makes me feel safe. No doubt, no distractions, no background programming, no thoughts. Confident, relaxed, and grounded.

M: Ask your future self how you achieved this sensation: confident, relaxed, grounded ...

S: I set filters to feel safe and stop making up situations or giving fear a chance to rise. The filters are very easy to set. He [her guide] shows me how. In fact, he says he'll show me how to set one right now. He says I can command. Look at him and learn to command the filter to be set. He says I can do it. He can't do it to me. I have to choose to do it. I know that I can do it. Okay, I choose to do it. There is no reason not to! Learning from him now. I have to feel that I am safe. At home I can set a reminder for myself to feel safe. Wear a ring to remind yourself. Oh, I know just the ring I have at home! Put a ring around yourself, your house, your computer, and your community.

She paused.

S: I have become sparkly, shiny, like a golden ring. I feel very comfortable with this new feeling of being safe. There is nothing to be afraid of. No one is after me or anything. I am all free. I am free.

M: What does it do for you to be free?

S: Oh, I feel I can do anything. Like this, I can do anything I want. Even things I need to do become things I want to do.

M: Where are you?

S: I am in the place of love.

M: Where is that?

S: It's me. Me. I am inside the whole world of *me*! It is amazing. I feel so free.

Her face lit up, and her posture straightened. She sat up in her chair, looking up, leaning slightly forward. I asked what she was experiencing.

S: I am guided to meditate as I used to before. It was a good way to relax, center my mind, and feel good. Also, now as relaxed as I am, I am clear that I have to take the next step. I feel an urge to move forward. The light will help me. I know it. I just know it.

## Staying in the Light for Life Energy

Tom was forty-nine and experiencing a bit of a slowdown in his life energy. He was a successful writer, and his wife had just had their fourth baby. Tom had always believed in a magic of spirituality. Now he wanted more energy to sustain his successes and feel more in control of his life. He relayed his experience and conversation with his guide as it unfolded.

T: I am at the mountaintop. The guide's name is Michael, in a whitish gown, youngish face. I am curious. He says, "You have a long life ahead of you." He says, "Just live within the energy of love." I ask him what this means. He says, "Just be there, present in your day. Just be the force of love, let go of the hurt, remember the loving moments, forgive yourself, stop the resentment, accept yourself as you are, and let go of trying to control. Agree that the past belongs to the past. Now rest."

T: I am resting, waiting. I feel very relaxed, and as I rest, breathe, and relax, the next level of brightness comes over me. I feel my body coming alive with warm energy surging through my body, up from my feet and down from my head. I feel every part of my body again, like my body was asleep and woke up in a whole new way! I am relaxed and calm and feel energy and clarity. I can't explain … It is like having taken a cold shower. Feeling fully alive, I feel light coming out of my body. Sparkling, clean, and energized. I need to go back to taking a cold shower in the morning to boost my body for the day. Also, I have to go back to playing piano and be more reflective. It would be good for me. I feel light. I am in the light and more energized.

Then Tom reflected with an observation.

T: It is really interesting how white the light becomes if I let go and relax. Clean and clear. Transparent. Really a new appreciation of life right now, how deeply I am grateful for this learning to be in the light.

## Light for Fulfilling Yourself

Terry was a forty-four-year-old business coach. She felt that creativity in her workshops and breakout sessions with her corporate clients had stalled. Her self-worth was dissolving. She needed a boost in inspiration to be effective at a new level of her creativity. We worked for an hour, and suddenly she made an announcement.

T: I am showered with light, and I have a strong sensation of someone loving me. Who? Doesn't matter. I am being loved. I know that I am being loved, and I am worthy of it. All that other stuff I wanted to ask doesn't matter now. I just want to feel this love. I deserve love, and I want to give it to myself, saturate myself with it. Once I am saturated with love, I am that which I want to be. I can sustain this by just thinking that I am loved. Oh, I know with confidence that it is true. Nothing has even been truer for me than this feeling of being loved. Then I can do anything I want.

## Stay in the Light to Accomplish More

Eddy was a talented computer engineer working on creating incredible unique "sequences" for a computer gaming corporation. He spent a lot of time in front of a computer. A lot of this time was fun for him, just playing games. It also gave him ideas for new sequences and made him a successful programmer. Because he spent almost all of his time in front of the computer, at thirty-five, his social and family life was almost nil. Eddy had become sad and was losing faith in his potential. His forgot family functions, holidays, dates. He didn't have this problem only with family; he had recently missed some important meetings at work, loosing track of time at the computer, jeopardizing his success. He was under pressure from his family to start his own family, and he was looking to uncover his potential in battling his computer gaming addiction.

His revelations were grandiose in comparison to the activity that normally went on in his life. At the same time, if Eddy refused the advice from his wisdom guide, nothing would change; no disaster would happen, as a negative future has never been suggested by a spiritual guide in a session. It was simply understood that the seeker would incorporate the guidance advice, make the necessary changes in his behavior, and take action to implement them.

The suggestion of a future where life degenerates is simply nonexistent. No journeyers with whom I have ever worked in the higher awareness have experienced any kind of threat of the end of life. Yet it is quite empowering to witness the profound persistent and personal reiterations that a person's life is in his or her own hands and that he or she has to metaphorically "get up," awaken, and take action. The sensation of just knowing without knowing is persistent and clear.

E: An empowering feeling of light is in front of me. This is my guide. He was a real person. I knew him. He was the brother of my grandmother on my mother's side. I see his thick wig of dark hair. He had been married many times. In a dark cheap suit, like a gangster, he stands opposite me. His name is Aaron. He says, "Take it easy. Life does not need to be a constant struggle. You can do more." He is smiling.

The metaphor of the gangster was powerful. The great uncle appeared as a gangster only to establish the image of strength associated in Eddy's mind with Hollywood portrayal in his favorite movie, *The Godfather*. Later Eddy told me that Aaron wasn't gangster-looking in life at all. The impression of him that Eddy remembered was that he was charming and smooth and very easy-going. This image was enhanced by strength of a powerful personality, a little grotesque but harmlessly creative in its influence on Eddy.

I asked Eddy to communicate with Aaron to learn his charm.

E: I ask, "What is your secret with women?" He says, "Be cheeky, arrogant." He shows me a hairy arm with a golden wrist watch and a glass of wine. Middle Eastern gangster image. What does it mean? It means power. He is powerful inside himself. Women follow this power. He is charming. I am not charming. I am inside and insecure. I am weak with women. They don't like me because I don't like myself. He is telling me that if you want something you need to exude good vibrations. I must like myself, and for this I must accept who I am. Who am I? Really, I am a gamer. I create games. I like leading people to labyrinths of intellectual play. I like to play. So be playful in life too. I like to play. I am childlike. I am happy, joyful, and creative in my fantasy. Create my fantasy. Create the fantasy that I want to have in my life because I live in a fantasy world anyway. Why not have the fantasy I want? He says I must be like this all the time. Come out and meet people in person. Not hide behind Facebook. Facebook profile is a confident place. How about real life, love, laughter—in person, not on the computer, not texting *LOL*. Look into a person's eyes. When I am gangster inside me, I am confident. Not really a gangster. Being a gangster is just force. For me, a gangster is strength. Suddenly Aaron has changed his image as soon as I made that connection, and now I see him as a rock star, a guitar player. He is on stage. I have never been on stage. It is live, like a live concert on stage. Cannot alter or change after it happens. This is not a recording. Life is paying live. Now he comes off stage to talk to me. He says, "What do you really want?"

Eddy went silent. I guided further.

M: What do you say to him?

E: I don't say anything. I don't know what I want. He says, "What do you plan to do with your life?" I say, "Live it. What else am I supposed to do with it?" He says, "Live it!" I say, "Am I not living it now?" He says, "No! You are wasting moments, opportunities, chances."

M: Ask him what this means to live your life.

E: He says, "Just seize it. Take it to your advantage. Get excited about an idea. You need to dare. Not hesitate or think too much.

I challenged Eddy.

M: Ask him, "Why bother?" You can have a life of a successful programmer without any other responsibilities.

Here I asked provocative questions to take him deeper into the experience.

E: Maybe it's my lesson—to dare … Otherwise, it's lame! My life is not full of life. Aaron says, "Live. Grab it by the balls."

I continued to challenge him.

M: What about your depression?

E: He says, "You need to maintain the strength. Otherwise, you will fall."

M: Is it physical or some other strength he is talking about?

E: No, in the mind. I need cocaine for the thoughts— in a metaphorical sense of course. "If you want to become me," he says, "powerful and focused with clarity, you need to exercise the power in your mind: positive thinking, strength in mind. Like using a muscle, learn to direct your life with your mind. Something to do, something to live for. You can dare to dream and implement your dreams and stop fighting with yourself and the world."

Before we began, Eddy had mentioned that he felt very discouraged about his attempting to step forward, and dating hadn't been as successful as he thought it would be. He explained that he had become afraid of failures. He called that being "slapped in the face."

M: But if you dare, life slaps you in the face!

E: He says, "So slap it back!"

He laughed at this comment from his guide. He went on laughing.

E: It feels good to laugh like this, carelessly, like nothing can go wrong.

M: Nothing can go wrong. It is all right.

E: Yes. For here you need a lot of power and energy. Keep motivated. Keep trying. He is charging me with energy now. In the center of my chest … I feel an infusion of energy. Laughing is powerful. Every time I laugh I will feel this infusion of energy. Now he is giving me a list of things to do in my everyday life.

M: Well?

E: Bicycling or skiing or running.

M: You have some bad habits that persist. What should you do with them?

E: Definitely say *no*!

I continued to challenge him.

M: But this is your routine!

E: Break out of it!

M: But how?

E: Just do it!

M: Does it feel good?

E: Feels great! I feel it! I am feeling it now. It feels great. I can get the strength. I want to get the strength. I can be strong. I am strong.

M: Is there something else?

E: He says, "Now listen to me about how to start a relationship with a woman. With a woman you have to be a man, sometimes dominating, sometimes soft, leading her to feel good about herself with you. Make her feel confident. You are a man. Find the right woman to have a relationship with and maintain it. In the relationship, you are a certain way about that person. Be genuine, be sincere, take interest, initiate things, take the responsibility for what you do. You can't throw it all at another person. You have to do it together. Together is a new way of yourself. It is awesome to share life with someone you love. Just do it! Instead of thinking too much, do something. At least something will happen to show you where to go next."

M: Aren't you afraid?

E: Aaron says, "I am with you."

M: How do you know if he is with you?

E: Just search for the feeling inside. Come on! Focus! Feeling in my chest showing me. I am excited, inspired, and it's okay. I am alive. All is well.

M: If you do this and change the way you live, where do you find yourself in five years?

E: Lovely house, lovely wife, kids. I am in control of whatever I am doing. I still do computer work. I love it, but now I do it intentionally. I am smart in my creative work. I am confident in my direction.

M: When do you start?

E: Start now. Stop wasting time.

M: What if you don't start now?

E: Nothing will happen. Everything will be the same, exactly as it always was. Everything will continue the same way as before. Dull. Sad. Unhappy. Longing for something else.

M: So what? Couldn't you continue like this?

E: But if you are alive, you have to make the best of it.

M: Who will help you make this change?

E: The guide says, "Certain decisions you need to

make on your own, like to start doing it. Then I will help you. You have to make this decision on your own."

I played the devil's advocate again.

M: Will you make this decision now? Or do you need help?

E: Quit joking around! Stop making excuses! Wow! It feels great to feel alive. Just go and do it.

## The Magic Pill

> *Life is like arriving late for a movie, having to figure out*
>
> *what was going on without bothering everybody with a lot of questions,*
>
> *and then being unexpectedly called away*
>
> *before you find out how it ends.*

—Joseph Campbell, *Creative Mythology: The Masks of God,* Vol. 4

Whether you are consciously aware of it or not, in your session you experience a separation from ordinary reality, which allows you to deepen your connection with your higher purpose.

This is being in the light. Staying in the light is when you have access to the light by being in the light all the time, choosing it at will.

Most people are willing to suffer and accept that the lives they have had and are having now are the templates for their futures and that they have nothing to look forward to.

By staying in the light, you step into the opportunity to break that cycle, to begin to create a new template of your choosing by easily and gently making the subtle changes in attitude and action that create a life in which your satisfaction and fulfillment are at least possible.

The sad truth is that most people are seeking a magic

pill or a simple answer, and they are unwilling to do what it takes to have what they want.

Yes, the magic pill or simple answer exist, but they are temporary fixes. They perpetuate your endless indulgence in fads and shiny objects that money can buy. And everyone is willing to admit that these behaviors are just temporary solutions to the realities of life.

I'm offering a lifelong answer to what seems to be everyone's desire for fulfillment and satisfaction, the feeling of feeling alive that most of my seekers tell me they want.

Those who are intellectually and emotionally equipped and those who understand that living a life with passion, feeling fully alive, rarely originates with one simple thing. It is usually found by those who are willing and able to master what it takes to get the desired results.

I am always eager to take on individuals who value the journey. Together, we create their journeys toward lives more fulfilling than they have ever had before or may think is possible while at the same time create sustainable stability in an unpredictable world.

Going inside to where the light is ... that's where I've most effectively helped others stay in their light and establish their connections with the future of the possibility of creating what they want.

## The Magic of Love

*When we strive to become better than we are, everything around us becomes better too.*

—Paulo Coelho, *The Alchemist*

### Light for Love

Anthony had been brought up Catholic and was struggling with a concept of God and truth. At age forty-eight, he was an established owner of an online business, providing for a family of five and a lifestyle of his dreams. Lately, he had been looking to make certain of his legacy, that he was doing the right thing, and that he mattered and was leaving a mark of his own in the history of the world. He was looking for his God.

M: Is there God?

A: Yes. God is different from what we all think or what we were taught. God created us to do the things we are destined to do.

M: Which things are those?

A: We need to love each other. Love your neighbor like yourself. It is a completely different meaning from what I learned in school. Suppose love is something bigger than just the emotion of love. Love is a life attitude. Love is a magic pill that you swallow every morning before you begin your day. Love makes you feel like you're God, and in this way, you are God. God is a source of creation, which you are too. You are creative, and you are God in that.

A: Love yourself. Love yourself means to take care of yourself so that you feel love, so that you look outside from within with love, and then things happen like magic. If you don't love yourself, you must start from the basics; they are simpler than we make it.

A: Love is around us. We are afraid to show ourselves. We must show it all the time. This is the thing that will heal us and will make the world better.

A: For me, when I hug my wife, I must first hug myself to know that I love myself, and in this way I love her. I love her for her, not for me. I love her because she is a good person and deserves to be loved. And I am lucky to be the guy to be chosen to show her how much she is loved. And she deserves to be loved, and I love her for that. And of course this gives me pleasure, and I love her for me because I feel pleasure from loving her. She loves me because I am a good person, and we give each other what we want to give—the love that each other wants. Our love toward each other is satisfying. It is just an idea: hug yourself, spend more time enjoying your life for yourself, and you will want to give more to others. This will make you more creative.

A: It's not about you or me specifically. Life is not about doing a particular thing. People think it is. People are running. People are missing stuff along the way. It does not matter what you do or where you apply yourself. You must have the creativity and the attitude, and you must be certain that you are doing the right thing for the better world. Real joy is not in doing the things you do. The real joy is doing things with love. Like being with the kids, wife, family ... Then you can't do wrong. Don't stop walking. Just stop running.

M: So what are you here to do?

A: What is my destiny? To be a good person every day, be in the everyday, even moments of the day ... It is not too much, just fulfilling my destiny. Ha-ha! I can feel it, how good it feels to fulfill my destiny, being a good person every day. Just stop worrying that things may go wrong. Purpose of life is to live. Being free to enjoy every day. Freeing myself from worry is the real freedom. To feel and to love. Yes, that's it.

M: So what's the secret to love?

A: It's not a matter of survival. Life is not meant to be a survival. It is a learning journey. We have to find the meaning in each moment. Otherwise, it's always a struggle. Even in luxury, it is a struggle of doubt and uncertainty. In love there is no uncertainty. You are with love, and it is guiding you.

M: So what's the meaning of life for you now?

A: Open my eyes to the life that I have. I am grateful for the peace and love in my family. I know I can make a difference in the world by bringing my energy to inspire other business owners and others who struggle with peace in their hearts. It is inspiring. I can feel it.

M: So if you knew what to do next, what would it be?

A: There are ways I can make it happen. I need to write it down and show it to the interested people, perhaps teach in a class or make it a book or both.

M: Who can help you in that?

A: I have connections that can help. I need to talk to people.

M: When you envision what and how this comes to life, play it as a movie in your mind, a movie about your future success.

A: I can see this happen very clearly. I know what to do next. There are a few things, also my company benefits. Well, I need to go now. I have everything that I need. Can you bring me back?

M: What about your other questions?

A: Next time. I am all clear now. I want to go and write a proposal now before it is gone out of my head.

M: It will stay with you. Moreover, it will become clearer to you how to do this as you stay connected to this moment, to the light, to this information in the benevolent way for all.

A: Thanks. That's exactly what I need. I am ready to go back to work now.

## How to Be in the Light

> *The cave you fear to enter holds the treasure you seek.*
>
> —Joseph Campbell

Jane was a youthful fifty-five-year-old technical writer. She lived comfortably with her husband in the suburbs. Her four kids were grown, and she was enjoying preparation to her retirement and assessing the successes she had achieved.

On the outside, she was successful and accomplished. However, on the inside she was lonely, sad, and inert, exploring issues of shyness, low self-esteem, and loneliness. Asking for anything was difficult for her, whether it was a promotion or a bill in a restaurant. It was amazing how successful she had become despite her secret low self-worth.

She did not have many friends. Although with those that she had, and particularly with her kids, she overcompensated by overextending herself, serving compassion, and lacking a sense of boundaries.

When Jane reached higher consciousness, she reported sensations of warmth and lightness in her body and a new and surprising sensation of being loved. She reported the awe and a connection with the inner divinity. She felt calm, safe, and relaxed while at the same time excited and buoyant. She spent a few long moments saturating herself with this new awareness.

She reported that she was transported upward and higher into the light. She was allowing herself to connect with what seemed to be a loving wave that was strongly and forcefully helping her achieve a particular height as she ascended. Along the way, she reported admiring picturesque mountains and valleys, whispering waterfalls, and colored skies and listening to melodies woven into the energy vibrations of color infusions and loving emotions. She described experiencing sensations of gliding through space and time. Her scenery unfolded quickly, and she reported back just as rapidly.

She became aware that she was moving through her life as an observer, as if she was watching slow-motion snippets of scenes from a fast-forwarded movie about her life. After each scene, when the event was over, she reported to have received instructions from her higher and authoritative guidance to release the past, and she took time to fulfill those instructions each time.

After she was done releasing, she reported feeling emotionally rejuvenated and a beautiful feeling of unconditional love streaming through her—a shower of light cleansing her as if she was a translucent vessel.

Most of my clients who experience releases like this have reported the feeling of unconditional love seemingly unavailable to them in their ordinary awareness but easily recognizable when accessing higher consciousness. The benefit of unconditional love gives them support in knowing they are not alone.

Jane became a vessel for the flow of love and light. Unable to control it, she experienced inner cleansing, which made her emotionally stronger and gave her a straightened posture and glowing smile. Jane was ready to receive answers to her questions now. The information came to her in pictures, sounds, and sensations that moved through her. She described her experience as reading an entertaining book or watching a movie about herself. She experienced a sensation of knowing, a sense of having been in this place years or ages before.

She described the awareness of eternity while at the same time having a strange sense of familiarity with the environment she was experiencing. After a bit of consideration, she found a word for it: "It is the home for my soul." She seemed relieved to have discovered it.

Jane connected to her wisdom and began to relay it to me. As I read to her the questions from her list relating to her soul, her family, her relationships, and curiosity about her personal legacy and contribution, she spoke as a representative of her guidance in a calm, soft yet advisory tone. She spoke the answers back to me as quickly as if she was reading them from a book. And what a book!

I asked her from where those answers came, and she replied as someone spoke through her, "From your guidance, of course." She mentioned briefly as a side note that she had heard herself speak and was surprised by the contents of her words. She discovered and admired the sense of humor and the benevolent love incorporated in every answer she received. The communication flowed freely and joyfully throughout her experience.

Then Jane began to spontaneously recite the inflow of positive suggestions she was receiving. The instruction came in a bulleted format as follows:

- Live with an open heart.

- Be true to your inner soul.

- Live in truth.

- Be conscious and aware.

- Delete old files.

- Be in alignment with your higher intention.

As her session went on, she elaborated on each point further.

M: Where are you now?

J: It's the kingdom of lights! I am wiping my feet at the door. Entering. Now … picture keeps changing … bright light, golden light. Here is a place to talk, with the lights off to my sides. A room golden and white. There are different levels, pillars …

As Jane continued her journey, she mentioned that the place looked strangely familiar even though she had never been there before, and it was definitely an imagined place because it had no floor.

Then there appeared her deceased mother. Even though she appeared to Jane a lot younger than the last time Jane had seen her—even younger than Jane—Jane recognized her mother's energy right away. Jane expressed her grievous hurt, resentment, and disappointment in their relationship. Jane felt her mother's energy embrace her. Emanating golden white light, her mother replied with the following words: "I love you. I've always loved you. You are loved."

This statement, "You are loved," repeated a few times during Jane's journey. Jane had a conversation with her mother, which revealed her mother's true and unconditional love. Her mother's love had been unexpressed throughout Jane's life per agreement both Jane and her mother decided on before Jane's life began. Jane had always thought she had been unwanted by her father, and now she found out that his contract had been to learn his own lessons. Her parents had done the best they could, and the struggle had not been about her but about their own process of learning.

This information took a load off Jane's shoulders. She felt relief in letting go of resentment toward her parents and reported a feeling of lightness and elevation. The process of letting go impacted Jane's transformation. With each moment in emotional connection with her inhibiting anchors, she integrated them and released the emotion associated with them, essentially freeing herself.

She let go of her preconceived impression of herself as a no good person. She had never confronted this identity as a reject even though she had taken years of conventional therapy. Now she was free and began to form a new concept of herself. The release of past limitation was supported by reintegrating former perceptions, coupled with my positive suggestions.

All suggestions were words that came from inner awareness and represented uninhibited freedom released through self-realization in her spiritual state. Jane expressed that she had never experienced anything as profound before; these directions from a wise place were exactly what she needed and never could have expected.

Furthermore, Jane discovered information about her life mission and about choosing her body and environment, which were suited for that mission, including choosing her parents. Tears of joy streamed down her face when she finally uncovered the purpose of her life.

Jane was eager to make changes in her life and left in a hurry. I haven't heard from her in two years. The following section contains some additional highlights from her revelations.

## What it's like In the Light

> *We save the world by being alive ourselves.*
>
> —Joseph Campbell

Sometimes, I ask questions for clarity and to make a philosophical point. It is not enough for me to know that the client received her guidance to stay in the light. I want her to question her guidance to know with clarity how she would benefit and how life would change for her to get what she wants if she sustains her connection to light.

For someone like Jane, who lacks appreciation or expression of love toward her, staying in the light would give her that connection to love, healing and transforming her own perception of herself.

M: What's the purpose of your being in the light?

J: The purpose of being in the light is to allow myself to feel the love. Every day and every time I do it, I see hands reaching out to me. I ask, "Whose hands are they?" In answer, I see light and energy. One light is brighter than the others, and I feel the higher presence of my guide.

M: Who is the presence?

J: I hear, "I am you. You are light. Be in the light."

M: What's the purpose for you to be in the light?

J: It's to feel loved.

M: And what do you want that for?

J: To live life and be productive in life. Like I am now,

it is just okay. I am just the corner mouse and do what I'm told. I was afraid to lose my humility if I am loved. I would just be more creative and assert my being if I feel the love that I am.

M: Tell me more.

J: I am a creative being. I am loving, and I am loved. I am free to express myself.

M: What's the best way for you to express yourself?

J: To dance, move around. Allow the music inside me to be heard.

M: Then what happens?

J: Then, dancing, I get ideas that make my other work productive.

M: Like what?

J: I am dancing now. I am dancing to my office. Light comes down and surrounds me, and I am plugging into the source. What a good feeling it is. It feels refreshing, replenishing. I just want to absorb this light. I am standing on a pedestal. Light is streaming through me, alongside me. And suddenly I know what to do next.

She was silent for almost a whole minute.

J: I am watching myself do my work. I am interested and doing it with love. I feel inspired. Those ideas I was thinking to implement a long time ago, why was I afraid? Now I know this is the right thing to do. It has been years since I was so inspired about it. I can see the faces of my colleagues … They smile at me. We are outside at a party. It is a party. It is a party on the job. The job is the party.

M: Tell me more. Explain what you mean by the party.

J: Partying is an attitude. You have fun at parties, right? I am having so much fun. I can feel I am plugged into the source. I can see I am walking above ground. So do others, particularly those who are effective. I can see Linda. She is my boss. She is struggling. She is not connected to the source. I can help her. Her cord is dropped. Let me connect her, see what happens. Wow, she is like a wound-up doll. Goes on at twice the speed now.

M: Seems easy for you. All you have to do is stay connected. And everything is easy. Isn't it true?

J: Yes, unbelievable. I couldn't have believed you if you told me it was that easy. But I have to do it every day, and I have to do it myself.

M: What do you have to do exactly? Describe it.

J: Everything, the city and all, came down to a small globe. Now it fits in my palm. The whole world is in the palm of my hand. My God, I am God! I feel like I am the center of creation. I am putting the globe into my heart. I become light. This is the best feeling.

She took another pause and then spoke again.

J: Wow, rays of light are now emanating from my heart. They are white gold. I am looking in the mirror. It is amazing that all I am is a glowing and flowing white light. We are all flowing wisps, very transparent. It is very bright light, a lot of light. Guardians are light too. I am a more solid light. They are more transparent. Guardians are all around us. They always are. I can see them in the mirror. They are waiting as if waiting for me to make a decision on where to go …

M: Ask them to take you to where you can ask your other questions, perhaps to the next level higher.

J: I feel fear coming up. I am hesitant.

M: Ask your guide to help you feel the fear evaporating from you and floating away.

J: Okay.

M: What is happening next?

J: I see fear floating away. It looks dark. Why would I have it? I am protected. Guardians are here to protect me. I am light. Nothing can change that. One of them is lighter. Taller light, beard, long white clothing. His role is to show me the way. He is saying, "Let go and relax. Breathe in the light." I am holding his hand and breathing. Then we are floating up.

J: Here are many people ... Mother saying, "I love you. I've always loved you." This feels good to know. It is very freeing. Emanating golden light, golden white light of peace and love. I am so grateful to know this.

J: Next is my father's energy—playful, smiley, laughing, hugging. "I love you. I never said it, but I love you." He is pale blue-white like an old photo, wavy hair ... He's got wings on. I ask, "Are you an angel?" He answers, "No, I put them on just for you!" He is funny. He put on the wings just so I would talk to him! I tell him I love him too, and I forgive him. My grandmother is here with her gentle smile. We never said much because she could not speak much English. Like then, we are holding hands and smiling at each other. She feels very solid, like a rock. I always liked that about her.

J: Now appearing is Mother Mary. Her role is to give me strength. We are floating in the light. It's just light now. We are floating through time and space, up and higher. We are entering a brighter light. I see crystals sparkling. I am overlooking the city. It is getting closer. A huge cathedral kind of door opens slowly into a large round room. White light streams at me from the opened door. This is a life room. I am looking at all lives I have lived, an archive of my lives.

M: What do you notice about those lives?

J: I always seemed to be outside of life. Like a narrator of events and people. I can see it now, in other times, in other lives. I need to be in the life, to be of life. In all those lives that are displayed now, I was alone. It's important to be of life so I can move on. What I didn't know in those lives is that this is my lesson, to learn to live the life I am living.

M: What does it mean? Can you not live the life you are living?

J: Well, to live a life means to be involved in it, fully experiencing all aspects of it. I have been shielding myself from emotional hurts and tried to avoid emotional investments in things other than family. I over compensated with family, giving them more than they needed, or wanted, being in their face, in their lives a bit too much. Emotionally and with heart, I had good intentions but from a wrong place. I thought I could be loved more if I gave more. But I didn't value myself. In other activities, like work, I participate like a drone, a robot, automaton, walking around like a zombie, afraid to invest my heart. I've missed much of life because I was too preoccupied with my own misery.

M: How does one become more of life?

J: I am more of life if I respond to an interest, a drive, a dream I have. Give this interest energy. I mean focus on it, give it life, emotion, time. Spend some time pursuing it. See where it takes me.

M: What is one of your interests that you need to spend some time pursuing, that perhaps you let go of in the past without pursuing it?

J: Working with my voice. I am a fair singer. I never gave it a chance. I need to take some time to pursue my voice. Find out what it is, what is my voice. Find my sound. The sound that comes from my core, that helps me find God within myself, to help me be with God. Be God. I am not sure why God comes into play here. I am not religious, but right now I feel that God is the closest representation of what I am experiencing. I don't need to be a singer but to find a voice as a teacher. To help open hearts to love. By teaching others but not in a classroom. Simply by sharing with others. Teaching others by showing up in the world by being myself. Being myself is a hardest part here. Why is it so hard to know how to be me?

M: What are the steps toward that?

She was silent for a while, took some deep breaths, and started speaking in a deep voice, with a tone of calm, authoritative persuasion.

J: Past your own resistance first. Live with an open heart. Be true. Live in truth, which is being aware more than I've been. Pay attention to little details in my own being, like what I feel, see, and hear, without judgment. Relax. Life is not a scarecrow. Laugh. Laughing is easy, and it is fun. Align with wisdom. Be less caught up in 3D, in everyday material reality. Be more mindful. Create the reality you need and want, and live it as if that is the truth. Feel and see love.

M: What do you need to do to be able to do that?

J: To find truth inside myself.

M: What is truth inside you?

J: Be more focused than scattered. Keep spirit with God. Always have this thought with me. To be of God.

M: How to be more of God?

J: Stop playing old tapes. Old tapes say, "I am not good enough." That's old. Not being loved, not deserving. Not being able to do it. Comparing myself to others who can do it better … New tapes say, "I am a magnificent being." I have the light. I am not alone. We are all one. Everyone is a student of life, learning to live the life with heart, fully every day. Everyone is a teacher. Including me.

M: What are you a teacher of?

J: I am a teacher of love. I am loved, and I am love. I live love. I exude love. I give love. I teach love. All else will follow.

M: What do you need to release?

J: Release old tapes. Really see the truth. There is no truth to be miserable. No one signs up to live a miserable life. We are here to learn lessons, derive teaching, live the life fully, expand, and create love and happiness. That's the real truth.

M: What is next for you?

J: Develop a cut-through vision for situations, like clairvoyance. See through the negativity. Does it serve anyone to be negative? Then turn the switch to positivity. The truth is to see that being of life is the only truth worth pursuing.

M: What is truth?

J: Knowing who we are, knowing our core. Who am I? We are all light at the core. And we are all one. We are here together. It is all one light. Light from source. We are all made from source. We must remember that and live it. This is the essence of life, to learn how to be the light and how to stay in the light. To connect the dots through being in the light. Light is a lens of life.

J: One can be dark and live the life of misery and regret, anger and indulgence. One can be light and live a completely different life of joy and love and have a positive approach to all things and beings, people and situations. Take all in stride with peace, not trying or forcing. With awareness that all is well and is designed to be well for the benevolent outcome. Everyone learns. Everyone.

J: I am here to help create awareness of bright light. All life is together. We are all made of the same matter. We are all from the source. We all come from the same place. We all have the ability to create things before things happen. Creating the things we want to create is the real skill. We all are here to learn this.

J: We can change what we create. What life used to be, what it was meant to be—peace and love—at the beginning of time, when it was not yet Earth, when spirit was here from source. Very bright here. It is a place of endless possibilities.

M: Ask for an exercise to bring back to your daily life through which you can re-energize yourself with light.

J: To infuse me with light, I can bring light back with me. To bring back this connection to light inside of me. The exercise is called, "How to be in the light." This is funny. I am shown a DVD version of it. You need to just hit the play button and start. I see myself sitting quietly and breathing, connecting to this place, bringing myself back for infusion. I am watching myself do it. It is easy. At the same time, I can feel myself experiencing it. I am both watching myself and experiencing myself from within. I am watching the higher version of myself do it first so I learn, like from a yoga instructor. I am now overflowing with light. The more I do it, the more light I have. The more I do it, the more I become merged with the instructor version of myself. I can do it when I want to reconnect.

M: Why is it important to do this exercise?

J: This is the time of change. I am part of this change. I have to partake in this change. I must be prepared. I need to take this exercise and teach it to others.

M: What is the message from your guidance?

J: Trust that I have everything I need to have the life I want. Life is easy when I start being in the light all the time, when I live from light, with and through love, in nonjudgment, and when I let go of my silly worries and fears that something could go wrong. Start doing the work, feeling free. Then there is not struggle; there is just a choice to be fully happy or not, and I choose happiness.

## There Is Only One Light

*Life has no meaning. Each of us has meaning and we bring it to life.*

*It is a waste to be asking the question when you are the answer.*

—Joseph Campbell

Harita is a thirty-four-year-old beauty with long, thick hair and almond-shaped eyes. She and her twin sister Geetika were brought to America by their unmarried mother when they were still babies. Harita's career in investment banking was successful but not fully satisfying to her. She had just entered into an arranged long-distance marriage with a banker working in Chicago but had remained in New York with her lifestyle unchanged. Her questions were about her lifelong quest related to her body image;

being good enough; longing for something more, deeper, more satisfying; her true self; and her life purpose.

Harita transitioned from being slouchy and uncomfortable in her seat to being upright and excited. As she connected with her place of wisdom, she wiggled in her seat with anticipation. The experience filled her with inspiration, motivation, and connection with the teaching about it, and it poured from within her. With deep emotion, she realized the curtain was rising, revealing her light and her own truth. Her concerns about her body image dissolved. Her experience of herself as a source of creation, as God, had nothing to do with her religious views. Having been brought up in a traditional way, she began to connect with her own uniqueness, her own symbology, and her own sacred inner truth.

M: Tell about your current experience of light.

H: Oh my God, I feel God, something really good. I am really godly! Like I am downloading God into me. Now I know I am God. I have God within me. I am sacred. I have to take care of myself as I take care of my altar, treat myself with care, respect my body, and respect everything that goes into it. All food needs to be sacred and prepared with love for me if it goes into me, because there is God inside me. It feels weird but a good weird. Very inspiring. Very profound. Unusual. I never felt this way. I have never had anything this profound. Even during a prayer. I can pray differently now. This is a deeper, more meaningful experience.

H: I am feeling so close to my parents and grandmother. It is inspirational. I see how we are all connected. I see what they meant to give me, and I have been refusing because I thought it was something they wanted me to do. I couldn't understand why. It's like a leap onto the next level, skipping a year in class. This is indescribable peace and calmness and happiness now. It is so inspiring for me to be myself in the best intention, my best me. I just want to be like this all the time from now on so I can live this inspirational feeling every moment. I know it is possible. It feels so good to be inspired like this.

M: Tell me, how did you end up with a body that is your body?

H: Of course, I picked my body myself. It is plump, shapely, and lovable. It is suitable for the freedom I have and what I came here to experience. I am strong, and I am independent. I am healthy and stand on my own. I just need to take care of myself. I am learning love, and loving myself is the start.

M: What does it mean to love yourself?

H: My body is a vehicle for my life. In order for me to fulfill my purpose and be productive in working toward it, I must take care of my body.

M: How do you do that?

H: I eat right. Fill myself with food that is nutritious, fresh, good, well prepared, and filled with vitamins and minerals. I eat slowly and in small amounts. I don't have to rush through meals or stuff myself. There is plenty of food around. I take time to eat right what is right for me. Stop eating snacks and sugary treats! Normally I love those! Right now I feel that that's exactly what I am going to do. I want to do things right for my body.

M: Is there anything else?

H: Oh, yes! Of course, besides changing my eating habits, I exercise, get enough sleep … I feel that it is easy, and I almost wonder why I didn't do that before.

M: Why didn't you do that before?

H: I feel that I didn't understand that this is what I wanted! Now I know that this is what I want. I want to be agile and flexible, and I need my body to function. I want to experience desire. I feel how wonderful it is to desire and be desired. I feel that as soon as I do things right for my body, I will have a better attitude and thoughts, and a commitment to my other goals will follow. All I have to do is stay connected to this inspiration.

M: How do you stay connected?

H: Easy, just remember this and choose this. I know my life will change now. Oh, I have no doubt. I am a changed person. I can't wait to live it and see what comes next!

M: What if your connection loosens? What if you don't remember or decide otherwise?

H: I will have to reconnect. Oh, I am so certain I can do it. There is no other way! Other ways are boring and dull, gradual dying. I don't want to die. I want to live, fully and actively. I am married, and I have an inspiration to live. I already decided to do that. We all can do it. I have to go and teach everybody that it is easy to do. It comes from light. There is only one place—light or God or whatever you call it—that is a source of inspiration and life and excitement. My inspiration is inside. I can feel it. It is like one continuous vibration, a tone of heightened happiness. There is only one light. In every living being there is a source that is connected to the source of the others. We are all one light. All we have to do is stay in the light.

M: What can stop you from reconnecting?

H: Fear that I am around negative energy. But then there is twice the reason to reconnect with light. Being connected with light is really the only way of being fully alive in my body.

M: How do you start getting rid of fear?

H: I take this responsibility. I have to be fearless. It is easy, by the way, because I feel that all my fears are just worries about a potential threat; it's nothing real. I have a good life. I put focus on myself and breathe. I am protected, and I am strong. I can do this. When I put my curiosity to my doing, I can get it done. When I have light, I have energy. I am light myself, and then all I have to do is glide through life because like this I know everything I need to do, no questions. It is true love for myself when I do right for myself. Energy is just the right level. My own light is brightened.

M: What can you do like this?

H: Oh, I can do what I want. I can be like this, and I can do my work, and I can like what I do and even get better at it. My boss will probably like me more, and I can make more money. I see myself being like this, inspired at work. Oh my God, I don't have time to eat the snacks and hang out or be bored. I am interested in my project. Projects, yes, projects! I can't wait to go back to work.

M: What about your family? How will your relationship with your family benefit from you being like this?

H: My mother is definitely going to benefit. My sister and my brother. And my husband, yes, my husband! I can't wait to show him what I really am!

M: What else can you do like this?

H: Anything! I can live my life like this much more freely, with much more … impact. My heart is so big now, I can kiss the earth. It would be lazy of me not to be like this. I know I am not lazy. I can make a difference. I will make a difference being like this!

M: Are you committed to being like this?

H: Definitely committed. I see myself being like this for real.

## Choose to Sustain the Light

> *The big question is whether you are going to be able to*
>
> *say a hearty yes to your adventure.*
>
> —Joseph Campbell

As part of my commitment to myself and my work, I live the philosophy I promote. I embody the uncompromising idea to live by the light. Over the years, I have noticed that daily contemplations on my intention of staying in the light, my connection with my personal reservoir of wisdom, and my conscious enhancement of physical activities in my daily life elevate my attitude and my effectiveness in my commitments. My work with clients benefits especially from my being the embodiment of light. In connection to others, I use a highly acute awareness of myself in my client's space as a guide.

My experiencing the flow of light in my body brings tingling to my extremities and warmth, even heat, all over my body with swirls, awakening my spinning energy centers and reactivating my chakras. At the same time, I experience tremendous relaxation to the extent of stillness in each muscle. My nerves are calm. My physical body is relaxed yet energized. My brain slows down and enters into a mode of creativity. Over the years I have done some of my most creative work after contemplation like this. My connection with the flow of light and the connection with my guidance happens instantly.

One morning after my personal connection to light and wisdom contemplation session, I experienced a tremendous heaviness and disconcerting agitation returning to the energy in the environment; it reminded me of swampy mud. This draining sensation was choking. I felt like I was tied up in my movement, unable to control my survival.

As an expert, I know that sometimes returning from the purity of light to daily activities feels heavy, limiting, and … physical. Yet we are physical beings, and living in our bodies, not outside them, is the reason we are here.

People ask, "How do I sustain the spirit of love and connection for myself and others?" The answer from wisdom always comes quickly: "Stay in the light." Staying in the light is an experience of love, connection, and peace. Learning to stay in the light and live in the light is the way to experience freedom.

For the experience of connection to your inner reservoir of wisdom to stay with you, you need to know that it is simply the choice of making the connection. All the strategies, advice, and guidance remain just an experience of the series of images, sensations, and knowledge in the non-ordinary reality, and you must choose to apply it in daily life in order for your life to be different. The daily application is a check of your connection to yourself, your inner wisdom, and your intention, and it is indeed staying in the light.

What is so real to you in your spiritual experience in your daily life, coupled with your intention, purpose, and guidance, escalates into continuous connection throughout your day, making daily decisions easy.

Through time, it becomes easy for you to find your way, navigating through daily tasks. There are no more complaints, no more disappointments, no more regrets. The benefit of applying the guidance routinely helps you figure out what to assign to memory and what to let go. As your brain develops neuronal sequences, the sensations of well-being that have positive influences on health, life strategies, self-discovery, and decision-making tactics at home and at work improve.

Once you have experienced a divine connection, make sure it stays with you in your daily reality. Practice it, refer to it, and call it up. Decide to have an empowered experience of your life. It is that simple.

Here are some benefits of staying in the light examined through real experiences.

## Staying in the Light Eliminates Anger

Sheina was a forty-three-year-old housewife living a life of her dreams in a spacious apartment in an affluent area of Manhattan. She was a mother of two teenage kids and a beginner entrepreneur. Her husband, who was a bit older, loved her very deeply in their marriage of fifteen years. Seemingly all was in place. She complained that in her day she often struggled between extremes of joy and lows of nervousness, feeling on top of the world with happiness and then noticing her own aggravation and doubt and distress over her perfect life. Life was too perfect. It was cloying. Sheina was a bird in the gilded cage. Even her weekly Sunday lunches with her girlfriends did not give her pleasure anymore. She exhibited agitations, temper, and lack of focus. She had started to put on weight.

"I struggle constantly with letting go of loneliness and being self-reliant," she noted. "I know how to enjoy life, how to be happy, yet I often choose not to. I want to stop that and choose happiness again."

She told me how she used to bask in the sunshine on the beaches of the Far East, where she had spent her youth. She longed for a sensation of doing the right thing with her life, basking in the light.

I explained that wanting to feel or do something wasn't all of it. The important part was to take action. We are our behavior. The way we express ourselves is the way we know ourselves and the way others see us.

If we choose to be sad, we act that way. We move slowly with our heads down. Nothing looks or feels good to us in this condition.

If we choose to feel happy, we are energized. We look joyfully up to people and smile. Sheina liked to smile. She felt good smiling.

I asked why she didn't smile more in her life. She said there wasn't anything to smile about. Yet she continued to smiling, because by then she felt good and the connection with the feel good was so strong that she just could not switch back to her inhibitory default. Yet the words that came out were driven by inertia of her preconceived perception. Now I had to anchor the feel-good position so she could sustain it.

We express ourselves in the way we take care of ourselves, so whether we rest enough, eat nutritious foods, exercise regularly, drive the clarity of our communication with ourselves and with others. If we do what we love, we experience purposfullness in our lives. Our expression is also largely dependent on what we habituate into our behavior from others in our environment, sometimes even as far back as our childhoods.

Sheina's mother was melancholic. For years, without knowing it, Sheina acted like her mother, sad and complaining, attracting attention by sulking over a menial thing or even making herself sick so her husband would pay attention to her. Lately her sadness had escalated to outbursts of anger because being sad or sick no longer gave her desirable attention. She wanted more attention but on a different premise. She wanted love and light, yet she wanted a different way to be in it.

Sheina's wisdom guidance was there all along. She was familiar with her guides, calling them in, listening to their communications coming from the depth of her wisdom.

Her questions were about the next step. How to rekindle her marriage, ignite a spark in her life, experience joy again.

S: I am my soul now … I feel bigger and taller than I normally am. Oh, now I am in my home and feel I am bigger than my body. It feels that everything is easier. I can change anything I want. Wow! Nothing is written! Daily stuff is not that important. It is important to be light! Love, the word *love* is glowing in front of me … Then love feels deeper. Then food tastes better. Flowers from my palms grow like in the spring. I hear a voice repeating, "Remember this! Like this, nothing can hold you back."

M: What's a better way for you to remember this?

S: If I forget this, I will be reminded because without it life is a dull repetition of movements, of daily routine: go here, go there, buy this, buy that, pick up after the kids, call husband. Like a machine. Now I can feel alive inside. It is unforgettable. I remember because it would feel different without this. If I forget this, I will be reminded.

M: How will you remind yourself?

S: Just sit quietly. Go to where nothing is going on. Nothing except quiet.

M: So you have to sit quietly or find somewhere where it is quiet. What if you don't get a chance to find the quiet place?

S: Let me ask that. You ask a good question. I need to know the answer. It doesn't have to be so quiet on the outside. This is a place inside me where I can find stillness, peace, and deep quiet. This is my place where the wisdom comes from. It is me. It is inside.

M: How do you reach that place?

S: Oh, I have to be devoted. I find time to practice while being calm, to be connected to this place where the light is. Then all becomes easy. I can see myself through time. There is no time. Funny but it's true; there is no time. Time does not exist. People created time so they could put off the things they want to do and do the things others tell them to do first. That's a backward system.

M: What's a forward system?

S: Things I need to do become things I want to do. I want to do things I need to do.

M: So what has to be true for that to be true?

S: I am like this—connected and calm. I am going to walk around like this and do my daily things like this.

M: What about your occasional angry outbursts?

S: Laugh more. Anchor this moment, the deep pulsating emptiness. It is so restful, and it is the core of life. From this arises light. Light creates love. Life is in the body. I feel weightless in my body now. It is a mistake that people think that being out of our bodies feels good. I can't experience anything if I don't have this body. It is only in this body that I can experience life. I have to take care of my body. I can see the connection now. I feel myself inside my body. I feel light-weightless and light-energized, and it feels so good. Oh, I feel so good now!

M: There is a business deal you are working on. How should you go about it?

S: I hear the voice: "Please don't do it for yourself!"

M: How do you need to go about it?

S: "Do it for the good of all. If you do it for yourself, nothing will come of it." For myself, meaning the selfish me. Selfish is good, but in this case I want to consider a benevolent outcome for the community. I have to do it for myself when I am myself; then it will be for the other. When it is for the other, I will benefit. So actually, it is for me but not initially.

M: What is your guidance regarding your relationship?

S: Give love. I am here to give love. I feel rather uncomfortable with myself not giving love because it's not me when I am angry or tired. I am myself when I am happy and joyful. So I have to be. Be ... but be exactly this way, with connection to light, staying in the light, with love. When you love someone, you love yourself. When you love yourself, it is the whole world that you love inside you. Then love comes out of you. You can't hold it inside. It seeps out like the juices in the core of a tree ... I am a tree, the whole tree—fruits, flowers, leaves, branches, trunk, and roots. I am whole. I am the whole world. Yet I am me.

## Connect with Light Source

*Your sacred space is where you can find yourself over and over again.*

—Joseph Campbell

You may appreciate the following exercise given to Lisa by her guidance during her session. In three simple steps, one can attain a peace of mind and connect with the light.

M: Ask to be shown the exercise to bring you back so you can know what to do to connect with light daily.

L: It is simple. Just follow a flow of energy. Direct

it to your breath, deepening it, centering your body in creating physically symmetrical balance. I can see it like I sit or stand, like that diagram figure on the poster in my acupuncturist's office. Very straight and balanced, both feet touch the ground, and my hands are at my sides. Comfortable. Settle inside myself. Quiet my mind. Deeply breathe in and out.

L: Then notice the golden light coming from the source to connect me to it. Perceive it. Invite it. Quickly I am taken to the light. I am here and there at the same time. I am me, and I am the source. I am here in my body, and I am the source of all knowledge at the same time. Stay quiet and observe in the light. The teaching comes very quickly. The communication lane is established. It is extremely clear. You should try it.

# Exercise for Your Connection with the Light

*Go out in to the forest and stay really quiet.*

*You will realize that you are connected with everything.*

-Alan Watts

Lisa's guidance gave her the steps to connect and be in the light. I am now passing this along to you, so you too have a clear and concise steps reference for your own use.

### Step 1:

Get comfortable. Take a few deep breaths to get centered. Take a few minutes or as long as you need to settle, connect with yourself, and quiet your mind. You can close your eyes or keep them open.

### Step 2:

Invite the golden light from above, from the source. Direct it to stream onto you. Immediately allow that light to bring you the sensations of love and peace, relaxation and quiet, covering you from top to bottom like a big feather-light sparkly blanket of energy, and let go of all unwanted energy right now. Allow the golden light to form a shield of healing protection and loving energy around you.

### Step 3:

Notice in the center of your body a spark of light ignited by the source light streaming through you. Allow that spark to shine outward, illuminating your way forward. Experience the empowering qualities of light. Quietly observe in your mind the light sparking outwardly from within your body. Merge with it. Be with it. Stay quiet for a few moments. Then return to your activities feeling great with positive intentions, energized, empowered, focused, and refreshed.

# Wisdom IX: Contribution and Legacy

*A hero is someone who has given his or her life to something bigger than oneself.*

—Joseph Campbell

## Meaning of Life

*Only those who have learned the power of sincere and selfless contribution experience life's deepest joy: true fulfillment.*

—Tony Robbins

My clients come to me when they start looking for meaning in their lives and find themselves in need of guidance. There is a way people want to express themselves for increased levels of efficiency and effortlessness in various areas in their lives. Particularly if they tasted success earlier and now want to recapture an idea to which they devoted earlier chapters of their lives.

By our early thirties, we begin to seek confirmation of our successes outside ourselves. We let the external markers validate our self-esteem. By our early forties, we look for the meaning of what we have achieved and confirmation that we are on the right path and confirmation of what the right way is. We begin to ask ourselves fundamental questions, seeking and sometimes not finding support in our long-held beliefs.

Who am I? Why am I here? What is my purpose? Am I on the right track? What is the right track, path, life? What was I supposed to be doing with my life? Am I doing it? Why is it not satisfying to just put one foot in front of the other?

John, thirty-three, was a fashion photographer and very connected with his spiritual guidance. In his travels all over the world, John had discovered many distractions from his work. He found that he was easily influenced by new friends, shiny fads, and others' opinions. His editor wanted more from him, yet John's interest was in creating art, not magazines. John's guide challenged his daily passivity toward fulfillment and satisfaction. Questions like "Whose life am I living?" emerged.

He received an instruction: "You can do more." John's first response was that it was too much effort to change for an elusive unknown. The spiritual guide persisted with the challenge, informing him that he was already uncomfortable and that it was bound to get worse. The spiritual message was, "Make a decision and commit to action toward living your life actively, intentionally, and in a self-directed way. One has to give up passivity, indecision, and apathy for action to take place. The result is satisfaction and fulfillment."

The suggestion was to take the next step, to begin to make art in his spare time as a hobby. John wanted to make a commitment to take this action. Unfortunately, the commitment to take action is often met with unconscious resistance because of old habits. He was used to going out with friends and distracting himself with other activities that interfered with his life intentions. John wanted to make changes, but he was often unable to follow through on his own. This is the reason some clients choose to have longer-term relationships with me. This way, old habits can be replaced with new and desired behaviors, which are generated in the higher consciousness space.

# Higher Consciousness Guidance vs. Traditional Coaching

*Immaturity is the incapacity to use one's intelligence without the guidance of another.*

—Immanuel Kant

The difference between what I am doing and the traditional coaching model is that new behaviors are discovered and driven through the higher consciousness experience as opposed to the traditional coach coming up with solutions for the client on a conscious level and installing solutions and behaviors often walled by unconscious resistance. My method gives the client a more self-initiated experience enhanced by the high level of their own readiness and places the responsibility on the seeker's shoulders. This is something many people missed in the transition from dependence to independence as they moved from adolescence into adulthood.

My model includes eliciting the client's higher consciousness connection with his or her original template, his or her own blueprint of success, and through a nonordinary reality the client initiates, opening the passageway to his or her future.

This is the space where the soul (also known as higher self, guide, guardian, God) and the everyday self (ego) can meet, unhurriedly take a closer look at each other, make an acquaintance, and discuss the perspectives, purposes, goals, intentions, terms, lessons, and conditions of the current life, past experiences, beliefs, and personal mythology within the path already taken and the path ahead. During that discussion in the wisdom space, we take a bird's eye view in recognition of what is important in fulfilling what we want out of life. We discover what beliefs are controlling our lives now and what needs to happen to create space to change. This is the place to get some answers to fundamental questions.

## Mission...Possible

*He who has a why to live for can bear almost any how.*

—Friedrich Nietzsche

When I came to my first spiritual experience, like everyone else I wanted to know my purpose, my mission. The experience started with my constant oscillation between conscious thought and curiosity to find out more. I quickly realized that in order for me to have the experience I wanted and to receive the information I was seeking from my higher awareness, I needed to shut down my mental chatter, interrupt my experience, and doubt my sensations. I was like many skeptics—overflowing with internal questions and judgment. I had to let go of my desire to understand and allow the magic to unfold.

As soon as I made the decision to let go of my analytical thoughts, I dropped into a very deep trance. I quickly began to have physical sensations of weightlessness and floating in my body. I lost awareness of the room, the facilitator, and the questions I brought in, and suddenly I had a curious vision. I noticed a floating sensation and observed a series of moving pictures as I watched the action from the inside, perceiving my body being in active motion while being still on the outside. I heard my voice speaking audibly with someone familiar, although on the physical plane I was motionless and quiet.

I began to zoom into the figures in front of me. I stood before an auditorium of nine people who looked like old men. They were uniformly dressed in white long belted gowns. Some wore glasses, and all were sitting behind a long semicircular table, facing me. Although I was in a place with no floor, there was a sensation of standing. A very bright light was shining in my face, and I experienced pleasant sensations of being loved and appreciated.

For a moment, I thought, *Nah, I am imagining this*, and immediately someone answered, saying, "Come on! Stop doubting! Be curious. Go on!" I brought my attention back to the scene.

Whose voice was that?

I had two inner voices: one positive, encouraging, and loving and one negating, complaining, and doubtful. When I questioned myself, I listened to who was responding. Another "me," a well-intentioned higher self who had a positive outlook for me undoubtedly answered this time.

The scene felt strangely familiar; I had no questions at this time about what it all meant. It felt like I already knew the answers to all the questions I was going to ask, so I paused quietly, admiring the clarity of this experience. There was certain acceptance in my awareness.

I felt loved, nurtured, safe, secure, and comforted. I needed nothing. I wanted nothing. I knew exactly that this was what I wanted. To be standing there. I looked at those old people and noticed one in the middle. He seemed more authoritative than the others.

The man winked and smiled at me. I noticed that in everyday life I normally wouldn't be able to see a person's expression from this distance, but I was clearly aware that he winked at me. I suddenly remembered what I had heard about the celestial sense of humor. Spiritual beings have a sprightly sense of humor and sometimes when we are too serious they remind us to have fun. As I've learned, spiritual guides remind us about life's pleasures with a childlike attitude or a humorous gesture. This was one of those moments. Yet I physically felt my eyebrows going up in surprise. As he put on his glasses (I was sure this was my conscious mind adding in the level of comfort in my perception), he looked through his papers, and then looking at me above his glasses, he said, "You are doing good. Yes, yes ... Bringing good. Good!" He put the papers down and looked at me directly.

There was nothing patronizing in his comment or the tone of his voice. I felt elated. I was doing good! In fact, in that moment I felt really proud of myself. *Wow, they are real!* my omnipresent conscious mind told me. *I have to remember this when I come back ...*

I then thought, *Here I am in front of the ...* I wasn't sure what to call them. I knew I was standing in front of the wisest consciousness in the universe, the collective unconscious, the bank of universal information, cosmos ... I did want this, didn't I? But for what? Wait ... Functionality of this experience is ... Questions, answers ... What did I want to ask here? ... Oh, yes ... The question: what is my purpose?

Though, in that moment it sounded sort of flat and irrelevant. *Purpose* is such a dull, one-sided word. There was so much more to what was happening, and the experience was so much richer to me than any words can describe. I thought, *Why do people look for answers when we already know the answers, because there are no questions to ask. Just have the experience and live in connection to light like this, and, oh my God, it feels so good!* I instantly had all the answers and knew how to be, what to do, and how to "fulfill the purpose," whatever it was.

I noticed that I was very deeply happy just standing there and experiencing that peace and love. I realized that like this, it was not possible to make a mistake.

"Purpose?" He said. "He-he, here ..."

I began to experience a multitude of sensations oscillating between feeling accomplished in my serving others, feeling peaceful in my heart, feeling free with no thoughts or worries, feeling loved and loving, and sympathizing with others and the rest of the world. I felt ready to give myself away to further service to others, to teach what's important so others could fulfill themselves, and to share what I knew, had, and possessed. In a fleeting moment, I felt vivid recollections back to the time when I felt most connected in my youth with my friends, when we all didn't have much but were a tight-knit group, and in the next moment I was taken by an overflowing sense of love for my mother, filled with forgiveness and gratitude.

The bright light around me became even brighter. There was a sense of tapping into universal wisdom. I felt the smallness and insignificance of myself in relation to the totality of what I was aware of. At the same time, there was a sense of my importance.

I felt the sense of responsibility that I was about to commit to something really big. It seemed as if it were an enormous sense of responsibility for all that I did, thought, said, and even the way I breathed. I was moving particles in the universe, and they also contained important information. Someday someone might need this information, so I had to be careful to put out only what was important. One breath, one step might decide the destiny of a much larger consideration—the cosmos, the whole world, and me, no matter how insignificant I was. At the same time, I was the most important thing in the universe because without me the experience of the universe would be altogether different.

The enormity of the experience was thrilling, exciting, and scary at the same time. I felt honored that I had been chosen for such high responsibility. Suddenly I became scared of that responsibility. It seemed that they had made a mistake assigning such a huge task to me.

One person cannot take all that responsibility!

Yes, surely I certainly could not have been chosen for this task with such enormous responsibility. I was just a human. I felt fragile and weak.

I felt I had to stop this mistake right then. It became

a very important issue. I screamed, "Wait! Stop! I can't! I don't … don't want it! It's too much! Take it away! It's not for me!" I cried and begged them to take it back and exchange it! Take it back and give me another task a couple of sizes smaller, like you would exchange clothes in a store. It seemed simple to do that. This was how it was supposed to be. Mine was smaller than that! Although it did not feel like the right thing to do, it seemed like the easiest thing to do.

As soon as I thought that—*Take it back!*—peace, silence, and slow motion suspended animation immediately came upon me. Silence rang in my ears. Blood pulsed against my temples. I could hear a butterfly flapping its wings. The sensation was that I was not my body and that I was a consciousness, although at the time I really didn't know what a consciousness was. I felt myself expanding beyond physical limit, bigger than the solar system, beyond the universe. I felt myself immediately suspended in a floating state, like I was everywhere and part of everything around me, accompanied by the liberating sensation of complete happiness, almost silly giddy laughter, and a peaceful loving sensation. I was basking in love. I was in a vacuum of happiness all by myself, all to myself. The only sensation filling this vacuum was a sense of suspended peace and happiness. Endless like eternity.

I basked in this happy state, and I was quite aware of the silence in the room at that point. I knew my facilitator was allowing me time for my experience and that the whole roomful of figures on the cloud in front of me also waited.

Meanwhile, I hung in that space of happiness and enjoyed myself. I had never felt so good before. This was better than any sensation I knew on a human plane. I thought to myself that this was the ultimate enlightenment … Yes, this was what I wanted. *This … is … what … I … want …*

I felt a warm sensation on my cheeks. They were wet and tingly. *Tears*, I thought. *Why?* Tears streamed down my cheeks, but I did not feel sad. It was accompanied by an awareness of unconditional peace, love, weightlessness, and bright light around me.

I finally felt in all fullness how much I was loved. I felt so loved. Finally I realized that I was loved for being me, not because I had done something awesome or deserved it in any way, but because I was me. And this was how it was. Simply, this was how it was. I was loved. Period.

I was enough. I didn't have to perform, jump through hoops, or wait for my mother to approve of me or for my boss to like me. I did not need to be promoted to feel better. I did not need more money. I had already gotten what I wanted—the awareness that I was enough.

I felt being a part of everything around me. I was part of all that there is.

I felt like I was floating, peaceful, and restful throughout my entire body. Suddenly I felt like I had let go of the trainload of dead weight, baggage, and garbage I had been pulling behind me all my life. I felt that life was good. It felt very good, so peaceful. At the same time, I felt I was floating rapidly through space and standing still. In front of me, I saw nothing more than just colors of red, purple, yellow, and white. I felt myself moving through an enormous distance, space without time, but at the same time, I was standing still. Yes, it was peaceful, quiet, silent. I now knew what it meant to be carefree. I wanted to stay there forever. I had never had such pure love before in my earthly life. I felt at home and at peace. Resolved and complete. Satisfied and settled. At home.

I felt I was just a little speck of dust. Dust. Yet an important speck of dust. Stardust. Star material. Part of what the universe is made of.

I could move my finger, and the rest of the universe would respond by moving some part of it too. I could say a word, and the rest of the universe would respond by creating something else, something new that gives life to something else in another form, and this begins an endless process of creating life.

I create life.

I am part of God, who creates life. I am God.

I had a feeling that I now wanted to create more life. I felt so important in the process of creation that without me there would be no particular creation, and I had to do what it took to fulfill what I must so that there would be the creation that needs to be there, because I am alive.

I had no idea how much time passed while I was having this experience. It must have been a lot. Ages. Years. On the other hand, time meant nothing where I was right then, so I had no idea how much time there was on Earth. I thought perhaps ten or even twenty or thirty minutes of the earthly time.

I went back to hanging in happiness. Suddenly it wasn't so great anymore. There was nothing to do, nothing to strive for. There was this continuous happy state in the heightened pleasure to the highest level of light possible. It was like a continuous mechanically repeated culmination that was replayed, and it lasted and lasted and lasted … I realized that this happiness had no purpose, no source, no mission, no creativity; it was just one continuous state of sameness, an almost exhausting, emptying feeling of culmination with no resolution. It was nothingness as this state. After a while, it felt like I was dead, and if I was not dead then I might as well have been, and when I was dead, I would be soon forgotten, and I hadn't done anything yet by which to be remembered.

*Why should you want to be remembered and by whom? Why is this important?* The questions floated in my mind.

Because I was a speck of stardust, and I could create by moving my finger or breathing. "Well? What do I create? What is my legacy?" I asked.

"What legacy? There is nothing to do. You are already at peace," was the answer.

Oh my God, I might as well have been dead.

My mind was ever so free. I had no thoughts. I felt so powerful.

Powerful in what? Doing nothing? Some power!

Powerful in nothing. It still felt good but no longer exciting.

My physical body was getting tired of being still. I wanted to move around, to feel alive. I was debating; it was as if two sides of me were struggling to find resolution about what to do next. Two very different directions. Just being happy does not exist, and it does not count. I had to fulfill myself, move, live my life!

"Couldn't I do it from here?" I asked.

"What can I do from there? I can't do anything physical from just being a soul. That's why I chose to be on Earth; otherwise, I can't do my mission. I can't "do" my life or give value to others ... Just hanging out there without a mission, is this what I want?" I was asking myself.

"Yes. This is what I want." It was still a very powerful and desirable sensation.

"Okay then," was the answer.

I was peaceful for a few more moments of suspended happiness, lasting and lasting.

Then I began to feel fed up with this pointless happy sensation of hanging there without any purpose, particularly the stuff that needed to be done on Earth. People were waiting for me. Life needed to go on. I wanted my life to go on. I began to feel that I needed to get back to start doing what I needed to be doing, what I loved to be doing, but then I was suspended in this slow-motion happiness that lingered like a gooey thick blob, enveloping me in its pleasurable sensations. It wasn't letting me go, and although it felt great, I was getting ready to make an effort to shake it off and move on.

I felt as if I was waking up to the life around me like Sleeping Beauty, like Venus arising from the sea. In the same instant, I knew I could not come back to Earth without a mission.

I was still without a mission. This realization shocked me.

I knew this much: without a mission one does not have any purpose on Earth. We come here to fulfill ourselves, our tasks. We are here to learn lessons, experience emotions, go through our lives in our physical bodies, living life to its fullest, with intention, and we all have to have a mission. I felt it in my body. I had to have my mission back, the one I had refused earlier.

More importantly, suddenly I realized that I was the only one who could fulfill my mission because I was the one who chose my own mission, this task on Earth that I now had to commit to fulfill.

My mission was so important that if I didn't take it, no other could do my part!

In that moment it became important to me that I get my mission back. So after a moment of hesitation, I humbly asked for my mission to be returned to me. "Okay," I said. "Give it back to me!"

I became aware of a heavy burden to be carried, like a truckload, coming down on me; the responsibility was dumped onto me, and my body immediately felt very heavy and physically pressed down. I felt like my bones were being crushed under their own weight, a ton of weight. I felt like I was never going to be able to feel light again.

But you know what? I felt so happy to have my mission back. Now it was mine! Now I was ready to do it! It felt precious to me now and not scary at all … My eyes were tearing once again as I felt grateful for this amazing experience. What could be more important than accepting my mission?

When I opened my eyes, the first word I said was,

"Wow!" And for a while it was the only word I could utter.

People who live in the light come to the realization that life has meaning and this meaning, this mission, this purpose answers a few simple questions: What can I contribute? What do I add to the value of others' experience of life?

## Meaning of Life Is Life

*We are in the free fall into the future.*

*Go ahead and do it playfully, the Universe is the God's play.*

—Joseph Campbell

Andre Agassi, a famous tennis player, speaks of his contribution in his autobiography. All his life he played tennis with a reluctant feeling because he didn't want to do other jobs, and tennis didn't give him pleasure. He spoke of agonizing hours and years of training and mechanical achievements and internal wondering about the purpose of the game.

Only after he created a foundation for children to support young tennis players was he able to feel the inspiration to be a leader, to be at service to others.

When one has everything, for a while it is new and exciting, and after a while it gets old. Take Oprah, fulfilling her purpose in serving others by living in the light, by supporting them in their efforts at being their best.

Often when I ask my clients what they want, ultimately they say that they want to be able to help others find their way, be themselves, fulfill themselves, etc. Yes, this is all good. But helping others does not start with others. Helping others starts with you. First you have to help yourself.

Clear your own stuff, straighten your own thoughts, gain positive awareness, learn skills of being in the light, and then embark of a journey of holding that space for others.

My mission to hold the light seemed too big yet very simple. Once I learned to hold my light, shining the light for others became easy. I have spent the last twelve years figuring it out. I have walked the path you want to walk. Now I offer to hold the light for others until they can do it for themselves.

## There Is More to Life than Sadness

*Remember that wherever your heart is, there you will find your treasure. You've got to find the treasure, so that everything you have learned along the way can make sense.*

—Paolo Coelho, *The Alchemist*

Linda, forty-four, was an accomplished self-employed real estate guru and online stock trader who had begun to look deeper into the meaning of her life in the past last year. Despite the wealth she had managed to amass, she was missing the feeling of fulfillment, meaning, and desire in her life. She wanted to feel alive, contribute to her community, help others, and share her life with someone.

Linda was not only a talented businessperson, but she was also a former model with a sad expression on her face. Things seemed to come to her, as she had achieved the markers of conventional success: a well-kept home in a gated community and stylish clothes. She commented, "I am sad because I feel stuck."

Linda was also very accomplished in her spiritual studies. She came with a set of symbols and mythology for her own transpersonal experience. Representations of her purpose emerged.

L: I see an image, a heavy wooden chest. I look inside. The chest has knowledge inside. I can't see it, but I know what's inside. Although I can see that the chest has a smooth finish and a white velvety interior, I am almost afraid to look inside because there is a very bright light. It's the light of knowledge … Knowledge is all there is. What is this knowledge? Knowledge of life, life represented by lines. Lines of life are all around me. My life and other people's lives are lines crossing or parallel each other. Knowledge of how to cross these lines is here. The wisdom is here.

M: Can you see your wisdom guides?

L: No, but I can feel their presence, and I can hear them speak.

M: Ask them about your task here, about your purpose.

L: I am here to remind myself and other people that there is more to life than sadness. The knowledge of life is in the chest.

To clarify the symbolism, let me explain. The chest represents a storehouse of knowledge. Our physical chests contain our hearts, the centers of our spiritual knowledge. What can she conclude from this? Her purpose is to follow the knowledge in her heart, live from the heart, and allow the intuitive process to take precedence.

L: I need to remind myself that there is joy, love, connection. My purpose is to be alive, to be lively, to live, to be their cheerleader, their inspiration.

M: How would you do that?

L: When I live inspiration, I can feel what to do. I am then further inspired. I do things with inspiration. I am joyful, filled with peace, yet energized and active in my life, and they can see that and are inspired by it. But I can't be sad and inspired at the same time. I have to give up sadness … After I decide to give up sadness, they [the guides] will give me concrete steps to take. This is the first.

M: How would your life be if you live from the inspiration as opposed to sadness?

Linda raised her head, straightened her back, took a deep breath, sat up, and spoke again.

L: Life is no longer a struggle between sadness and joy. It becomes joy. But I have to remember to be joyful. All aspects of life are real. We keep thinking that only what we believe is real. Not even that is real! Our position, our point of view, and our attitude make a difference in how real the reality that we experience is. Reminding us that this is real, all is real. All thoughts are real too. Good or bad ... Well, there isn't a good or a bad. People created good and bad qualifiers. Both are equally valid and serve a purpose. A different story is whose purpose or what purpose they serve. But both good and bad in the universe are the same source energy ... If it's not yet real, it becomes real as soon as you think it. Our planet is alive. It breathes. It has consciousness. And every stone is alive, as is a flower and a molecule of air. Everything offers a perspective from which to view our existence. It's necessary for energy transformation to go beyond what's seen, what's obvious. Then energy transmutation happens. There is no sadness, just energy that can be transmuted.

M: When you give up sadness, transmute it, then what happens?

L: It is then that I begin living in the place where there is no sadness. There is only inspiration. I want inspiration, and I don't want sadness. And that is my choice. It feels good to be here. I wish I could stay here. There is so much light, and everything seems easy. But I want to go back to living in my body, and I can stay connected. I am told that if I stay connected, I can come back for more inspiration anytime. To live inspiration instead of sadness. To give up sadness, I have to give up perfection. I think I am not perfect, but I am. I have to give up seeking perfection. I am already perfect. Wow, it is so easy and yet hard for me to believe. I can feel the calmness and the knowing that I am already perfect. I was born perfect. We are all born perfect.

L: I am an example. An inspiration for people to see and be inspired to live in their own way. There is an idea of a free will. In order to exercise free will, people must feel free to decide. They must be free to decide and then act on that decision. They must feel free to express themselves in the ways they want and need to express themselves. Most of the time we are not free. We are waiting to get an approval or a direction. This is not free will; this is the surrendering of the free will. We must find what makes us unique and emphasize that and create life around that. Then there is free will.

M: Why is it important to exercise free will?

L: We need to see the light in ourselves first. Then see the light in each person. We are not separate. We are together. We can influence each other's energy. The more light I am, the more light can be seen by others, and then they can be part of that light. It is difficult to keep dark when all around is light. Once I am free, you are free. Once you are free, I can be free also. Freedom is light. Light gets brighter when you are free.

M: What is this place where you are now?

L: It is a place of love.

M: Where is this place?

L: It is inside of me. It is me. I have a sensation of being free. This is the true me. I can't explain; it just is. I am free. I was born this way. Like a wisp of a cloud in the sky, I am a free-flowing energy. I feel relaxed. I feel spontaneous. Spontaneous in my expression. That's free. I sparkle like gold, like a star. I am pure sparkle. Laughing, smiling, talking with people, one person at a time. Giving energy to the space of another person for them to take if they need it; if they don't need it, my energy will be recycled. It is not my energy. I am just directing the energy of the universe flowing through me. Energy does not go to waste. Nothing is wasted. Everything is used. It's all good.

M: How is free will exercised in your career?

L: Healing comes up. I need to let go of the baggage. I am helping people organize their lives. I feel satisfied. Healing is a very broad word. I don't have to be a nurse or do a massage. There is more to it than just a massage table. I help people make decisions!

Notice the metaphor of healing coming up as a career, but the reflection on the symbolism brings healing back to Linda; self-healing and letting go become priority themes for her. Linda becomes an example. She has to decide how to live her life, and then her life will become exemplary to others. Others can decide to live free.

M: What should you do searching for a soul mate?

L: I feel sparkly in his presence.

Linda was shown the sensation she would experience in the presence of a soul mate and by which she would know he was the right person for her. Often people look to see an image or hear a description of their soul mate. For visual people, there will be an image, and for language-oriented, linear, auditory people, there may be a description with a list of character qualities. Not for Linda. In this case, she was kinesthetic, attuned to her feelings, her sensations. She was shown how she would experience her soul mate and what it would feel like to be in his presence.

L: I don't know who he is, but I will be recognizing my own experience of myself in the presence of my soul mate. This creates an opportunity for me to meet him. I am now open. I will be on the lookout to experience the same sparkly sensation. Just sparkly.

She must feel herself as a sparkle when she is next to that person.

M: What is your help in the community?

L: I see myself carrying books from the house to courtyard, talking to a female. This is part of my work.

I work in a vacation spot as an event planner, very comfortable. I don't have to work, but I want to. This is part of my skill-set that I can utilize to help my community. I have not considered being an event planner. This is interesting. I meet new people all the time. This is perfect for me. People come and go. We influence each other's lives ...

Linda's idea of work in the future was connected to people, community. Right now she was alone in all her activities. Right now, any work where she may be with others might be satisfying for her. Once she decided in that direction, she could connect to her guides to help her narrow it down.

M: What is your future self telling you?

L: She feels safe, fearless, standing tall with confidence, no second-guessing, relaxed, grounded, happy, checking her filters to feel safe and comfortable.

M: Do you like how she feels?

L: Oh yes. She feels very comfortable.

M: What's your next step to make that happen?

L: Meditate, set the filters, and start doing active work for the community. This is very satisfactory. I feel merging with my future self.

# Epilogue: Be Yourself

*Life is without meaning. You bring the meaning to it.*
*The meaning of life is whatever you ascribe it to be.*
*Being alive is the meaning.*

—Joseph Campbell

I have noticed that the emphasis on the wisdoms vary from person to person. Sometimes case history shows the whole list of nine wisdoms, and sometimes it shows just a few. For those individuals who have follow-up sessions in their mentoring processes, the emphases shifts through time. When a journey is updated two months or two years later, the emphasis is on what is important at the moment, after they have implemented the previously revealed wisdom.

The truths are there. Always presented in one way or another and fitting into the above described categories.

Individuals who acted upon the information they received from the wisdom found that their lives began to open up and be more fruitful. They found their satisfaction.

Those who didn't act upon the wisdom and didn't make the necessary changes found themselves continuing to search, long, and desire for the same sense of answers, unwilling to accept the wisdom they received. The wisdom of the transpersonal experience lives within all of us, endlessly pointing us in the direction of happiness and fulfillment.

The road map is there. All we need to do is unfold it and take the first steps toward the wisdom points.

## Commitment to Being Yourself

Salam was a forty-four-year-old CEO of a large Wall Street firm and a very attractive woman. She was looking for help being creative in her team as they worked on a new corporate project.

She shared, "Early on, because of some childhood circumstances, I was forced to be alone and grew to like being a loner. It is not the case now. I long to be with people and cannot bring myself to commit to trusting others. In my position, working with others mustn't be a struggle. I work in a team, and I have to exhibit leadership skills, yet I am shy and withdrawn."

As she reached her wisdom, the guides shared her desired image—confident, creative, and focused on the positive outcome.

M: Like that, how are you with people?

S: I see myself as a queen matriarch who bears responsibility of her duty in lonely solitude and brings outside an image of strong leader. My life makes sense now. I spent a lifetime feeling homesick for a place I couldn't put my finger on and longing for friends [my guides] who I was hoping would rediscover me. I was afraid to commit to being human, feel my body, and be in touch with my emotions. It seemed strange to have lost my way back to that elusive home. Now that I get it, my anxiety is completely gone. I couldn't get it if I wanted to. There is no reason to agonize. I see my home and my friends. They are my guardians, and my soul is at peace. I am not afraid anymore. I am at peace to have regained the ability to connect with them. They are my wisdom. I trust them. I can be who I am. I can live my life and be in connection and draw wisdom and light from here. What a wonderful moment of truth for me.

# Conclusion: Decide What To Do Next

*Action is a foundational key to all successes.*

—Pablo Picasso

## Take Action

*The big question is whether you are going to be able to say a hearty yes to your adventure.*

—Joseph Campbell

Many people are looking for purpose and meaning in their lives. They say it is important to know these answers.

In my experience, people are looking for wisdom about what to do next. The majority of my clients aren't looking for entertainment, although the undeniable aspect of mystical adventure of the space in between is obvious. They also want true depth and meaningful resolution in their quests.

Consider the following questions: Why is it important to you to know your meaning? What are you going to do with the information you receive? Are you prepared to take action on the instructions you receive from your guides?

Before you know the answers, your ignorance is excused. As you uncover the path, meaning, and purpose of your life and learn from your spiritual guidance the steps to fulfill yourself, along with the actions you need to take, you can't claim ignorance anymore. Now is decision time. Take action on those instructions from your guides, and you are on your way to meaningful fulfillment of your purpose. Ignore them, and life goes back to the old patterns, and the gnawing feeling of dissatisfaction with your life still remains.

## Positive Guidance to Action

*Action expresses priorities.*

—Mahatma Gandhi

In the last decade, I have worked with people from all walks of life: teachers, nurses, doctors, executives, assistants, directors, merchants, managers, entrepreneurs, professors, business owners, housewives. I have worked with men and women who have known success, who have tasted the sweetness of the good life. They come from all over the world: the United States, Canada, Russia, France, England, Spain, Austria, Australia, India, China, Taiwan, Japan, Egypt, and Israel.

What I have found is revealing. The lessons of the spiritual learning have been coming up uniformly in the direction of light and were primarily geared toward creating space to support courage of people who want to move forward and bring light to others, teach them, and help them to be in the light.

Nowhere in the meetings with spiritual journeyers that I have conducted over the last decade of my dedicated work have the lessons come up as guidance to hate the humanity or to care what other people say about you or to humiliate yourself, your loved ones, or co-workers. Not one session ever mentioned that you should sacrifice your personal integrity in the name of shareholder profitability. Not one instance of creating awareness was devoted to being untrue, compromising one's own life values in the name of making others' values the guideline to satisfaction, or disrespecting one's body or mind.

## Guidance from Light

> *An ounce of action is worth a ton of theory.*
>
> —Ralph Waldo Emerson

Here is what the guidance did say for people who ask the questions:

- The wisdom that comes through is the wisdom of compassion and human condition.

- Embrace the changes and transformation.

- Understand that it is all about this, and love the process.

- It's like breathing; it's the natural course of life.

- This is life in the universe; see an image of a butterfly.

- It's transformation. Accept that the purpose is to love the change and joy.

- It's the state of mind in everything we do.

- For your fulfillment in this life, get clear minded

and attuned to the right place, which is the place of light and love.

- That's the lesson, to find the right place and look inside.

- This is the right place.

This list is from Eric's session.

There is more, however. Let's not forget the conclusions in many sessions are based on the revelations and "ah-ha" moments, but there is always the next step: a decision to take action.

## Commitment to Take Action

*I've realized that being happy is a choice.*
*You never want to rub anybody the wrong way or*
*not be fun to be around, but you have to be happy.*
*When I get logical and I don't trust my instincts —*
*that's when I get in trouble.*

—Angelina Jolie

Anika had lived in an arranged marriage since she was nineteen. She was now thirty-nine. Before her marriage, she had been in love and still remembered her first boyfriend's caressing kisses. She loved her current husband, with whom she had three teenage kids and was happy on the outside. Inside, she was gnawed by the feeling of incomplete expression of her love. Her question to her guidance was whether to stay in or leave her marriage.

She connected with her guidance, which she called God. She said that she normally communicated with God all the time, but in the past few years, God had been giving her confusing messages. She wanted to uncover what it was about, how to trust her God, and what the next step was.

Connection with God was an easy one. They reconnected as good friends who hadn't seen each other for a while. Her guidance was simple: "Listen to your messages." I asked what it was about. She revealed the following.

A: I haven't been listening to my God, and even though I heard my guidance messages to give me directions, I either ignored them or did as I saw fit. However, I recognize now that what I thought was fit for the situation was just a weak, bad strategy and from a bad place. It wasn't a good decision for me to take the offer of the arranged marriage, but I did it for my father. I threw my life away to save my father's reputation. Now I am in it twenty years. What's next? What is my purpose with this man I married?

M: Ask your guidance to give you insight.

A: The answer is that I am here to stay and learn to give love. I am being shown a past life where I met my husband for the first time. He picked me up from the street where I was just a poor girl selling myself for living. My first boyfriend is in that past life too. I was married to him, and he was killed in the war. I could not bear that separation, and my love was left unexpressed. I became weak in the mind and lived in the street. Men took advantage of me. Women laughed at me. My current husband saw me and cleaned me up, and I lived with him until the end. But I never loved him as I loved my first boyfriend. There is a layer of awe and gratitude but not sensuality. Now I have to learn to live, love, and give love because love is the source of light, and there isn't anything else, just light and love. When one carries light, it is all love around them. And it feels good to be like that.

M: Could one learn to love someone?

A: One can learn to express the love he or she feels

inside themselves. Direct it to that person. He or she deserves to be loved. Just like we all do. I have love, and I was locking it in, holding it back like a hostage, keeping it from coming out because I am afraid of the emotion, of being hurt again. Now I know what to do.

M: What is the future of that?

A: I see myself sitting on the lap of my husband, and I can feel how happy we both are just being together. All I have to do is smile and be joyous. He loves me, and I love him. We are so happy together.

M: What about your social life, your friends, and other people?

A: When I am with love, I am light, just shining. Everyone can see my light. It is so rewarding to be that light, and it feels so good. I can't tell you how good I feel now. Oh, what a pleasure. Thank you for bringing me here to know this feeling. It is so motivating.

M: Will you do it?

A: What if I couldn't?

M: Like this, can you do it?

A: Yes, right now I can.

M: What do you need to continue that commitment?

A: I don't need anything else. Just my decision to stay with the light and give love as much as I want.

## What's Next?

> *Destiny is no matter of chance. It is a matter of choice.*
> *It is not a thing to be waited for, it is a thing to be achieved.*
>
> —Unknown

The experience of spiritual regression is so entertaining, so unusual, and so transformational that the changes it offers through its metaphorical format create profound personal and permanent transformation for each participant. Once we decide to take a lead in our lives and follow the guidelines of the wisdom we were offered, changes begin to take place.

I became interested in finding the brain science behind the changes that my sessions trigger in those who commit to taking action in the direction of their intentions. The brain research shows that the areas of the brain that are activated during the interactive meditation in wisdom states are related to visualization of the future and decision-making areas in the prefrontal cortex, along with motor cortex activated in the right side of the brain, indicating readiness to take action. This was encouraging to me, and I began to seek funding for new research with one of the New York hospitals to show that gamma hypnosis would be an easy way to make decisions and take action upon those decisions along the personal path of fulfillment and satisfaction.

## Guidance for Results

> *The artist alone sees spirits.*
> *But after he has told of their appearing to him,*
> *everybody sees them.*
> —Johann Wolfgang von Goethe

Tremendous changes happen in the lives of those who commit to following and staying in the light.

I receive notes from my clients describing relationships miraculously recreating themselves after months of no intimacy and threats of divorce. Within two days after a session a wife had with me, her husband "made a move" to reinstate intimacy with her, rekindling the flame of physical closeness, because her behavior had changed and allowed him to see her true intention in a new way.

Another client reported a successful upgrading of work. Yet another delivered a baby in peace and enjoyment. Still a third made changes in her work-home arrangements, accommodating her changing priorities with growing children and still enjoying business success.

Oftentimes, at first the decision may seem too difficult to act upon. There is too much to give up or too much to change. This illusion is only temporary. Once the transition starts, we can't stop the change. In order to get what you want, whatever prevented it from happening so far needs to end.

Frequently, upon your decision to stay in the light and be true to yourself, some relationships, jobs, or situations have to end. Other times, as the light shines on a perspective, the guidance shows ways to revive interest in the field or a relationship. It is all very personal and very specific.

What changes is the position from which decisions are made and the level of decisions. Decisions become higher-quality decisions, defining clarity without doubt, which brings a deeper experience of being alive.

Sometimes people walk away, delaying taking the action. They go back to their lives as before. They say, "I didn't do what I was told to do to free myself and live my life. I just did what I always did before that. It was impossible and difficult, and I was afraid." When such a decision happens, it seems that the world left them, and their guidance is no longer there.

But it is not so. The guidance is always there with us. When we go against it, the guides silence themselves, and it seems that we are alone.

Many forget that the light is for everyone. The truth is for everyone, but what you choose to do with it is for you to decide.

The guides make no demands on the person, and the door is always open. Change is a matter of choice through time.

The decision may have been taken on a different level—not to act, not do anything about it. That's a decision and an action too. Then you may need help from a person or mentor, and many of my clients enjoy walking with me through each step of the way. They know there is someone they can trust, who can walk with them until they can see how to do it on their own, who can mentor them through tough times and indecision and lead them to the threshold.

That decision to stay with the light is not a decision until the action is taken to do it. That is to decide to live in the light. The decision to live with light may remain a dream for a while until the person takes the first step. So the sooner you start, the sooner you begin to enjoy the benefits of satisfaction with your life.

And it is you who must cross that threshold alone, to where your guides are waiting for you endlessly. And that is where your journey really begins. The journey into the extraordinary life.

What occurs in the transpersonal light journey is experiences of personal uniqueness, creativity, fulfillment, empowerment, satisfaction, and love. The premise is both fulfilling and challenging. These experiences are, in fact, both worshiped and denied by our culture.

When people decide to explore their purpose and fulfillment, seeking how to make their lives even better, they look for a specialist, a catalyst for the experience of connection with the divine inside them.

Suddenly, the old means of dealing with their lives no longer work. There is a need for a change. There is a search for a renewed sense of purpose, meaning, and legacy. Notice a changing quality of your questions from "How can I get that?" to "How can I contribute?" and you have entered into the part of your life called maturity.

Sometimes we don't have the means to mature with time, or sometimes familiar means no longer work. Then we may be in need of an update to the means of being and need to uncover what creates the next part of our lives and leads to a very special point of satisfaction of being fully alive.

Everything suddenly comes to a stop until these fundamental questions are resolved: What am I here for? How can I make my life more fulfilling?

Until the confirmation is uncovered. What is my life intention? What is the right direction for me? Am I on the right track? What am I supposed to do now? How was I meant to contribute? Who am I?

So if lately you have found yourself asking fundamental questions about yourself, a transpersonal journey may be a way for you to get started. Seek to stay in the light. It's changed my life, the lives of my clients and it will change yours.

# Resources

For New York Awareness Center's philosophy, trainings, news and blogs as well as individual opportunities with Morrin Bass explore these links:

www.NewYorkAwarenessCenter.com
www.NewYorkAwareness.com

Morrin Bass' personal web-blogs:
http://www.MorrinBass.com

http://www.lifebetweenliveslbl.com
http://definelifepurpose.blogspot.com/
http://conversationswithhealingangels.blogspot.com

For group and corporate speaking engagements go to:
http://MorrinBassSpeaker.com

Write to Morrin Bass directly at:
newyorkawarenesscenter@gmail.com

# Bibliography

*Lewis Carroll, Alice's Adventures in Wonderland, Dover Thrift Editions, 1993*

*Joseph Campbell, with Bill Moyers, The Power of Myth, Doubleday, 1988*

*Joseph Campbell, The Hero with A Thousand Faces, Pantheon Books, 1949*

*Joseph Campbell, Pathways to Bliss, Mythology and Personal Transformation, New World Library, 2004*

*Joseph Campbell, Transformations Of Myths Through Time, Harper and Row, 1990*

*Joseph Campbell, The inner Reaches of Outer Space, Metaphor as Myth and As Religion, New World Library, 2002*

*Joseph Campbell, Myths To Live By, Compass Press, 1972*

*Joseph Campbell, Myths Of Light, Eastern Metaphors Of The Eternal, New World Library, 2003*

*Robert Graves, The Greek Myths, Penguin, 1955*

*Robert Dilts, Tim Hallbom & Suzi Smith, Beliefs, Pathways to Health & Well-being, Metamorpous Press, 1990*

*Shakti Gawain, Creative Visualization, Bantam Books, 1978*

*Norman Doidge, MD, The Brain That Changes Itself, 2007*

*Miguel Ruiz, The Four Agreements, The Practical Guide to Personal Freedom, (A Toltec Wisdom Book,) Amber-Allen Publishing, 1997*

*Joseph Riggio, PhD, The State of Perfection, Amazon Kindle, 2012*

*Daniel J. Siegel, The Developing Mind, Guilford Press, 1957*

*Victor Turner, The Ritual Process, Aldine De Gruyter, 1969*

*James Hollis, PhD, Finding Meaning In the Second Half Of Life, Gotham Books, 2005*

*Joyce C. Mills and Richard J. Crowley, and M. O. Ryan, Therapeutic Metaphors for Children and the Child Within, Bruno-Mazel, 1986*

*Thomas Hanna, Somatics, Reawakening the Mind's Control of Movement, Flexibility, and Health, Addison-Wesley Publishing, 1988*

*Richard Bandler and John Grinder, Patterns of the Hypnotic Techniques of Milton. H Erickson, Vol. 1-3, Meta Publications, 1975*

*Douglas De Long, Ancient Teachings For Beginners, Llewellyn, 2000*

*Robert Masters, Neurospeak, Transforms Your Body, While You Read, Quest Books, 1994*

*Carlos Castaneda, Journey to Ixtlan, The lessons of Don Juan, Pocket Book, 1974*

*Ted Andrews, The Art of Shapeshifting, Dragonhawk Publishing, 2005*

Dave Elman, Hypnotherapy, 1964

D. Corydon Hammond, (Editor) Handbook of Hypnotic Suggestions and Metaphors

Michael Heap BSc, MSc, PhD, Kottiyattil K. Aravind MBBS FRC, Hartland's Medical and Dental Hypnosis

Sidney Rosen, My Voice Will Go with You: The Teaching Tales of Milton H. Erickson

C. Roy Hunter, The Art of Hypnotherapy: Part II of Diversified Client-Centered Hypnosis, Based on the Teachings of Charles Tebbetts

Milton H. Erickson, Ernest L. Rossi, Experiencing Hypnosis: Therapeutic Approaches to Altered States

John Grinder, Richard Bandler, Frogs into Princes: Neuro Linguistic Programming, Real People Press, 1979

Martin L. Rossman, M.D., Guided Imagery for Self-Healing

David Gordon, Therapeutic Metaphors: Helping Others Through the Looking Glass

Michael Newton, Ph.D., Life Between Lives Hypnotherapy for Spiritual Regression, Llewellyn, 2004

Michael Newton, Ph.D., Destiny of Souls, Llewellyn, 2004

Michael Newton, Ph.D., Journey of Souls, Llewellyn, 2004

Dennis K. Chong and Jennifer K. Smith-Chong, Don't Ask Why? A book About The Structure Of Blame, Bad Communication And Miscommunication, C-Jade Publishing, 1991

Michael Harner, The Way Of The Shaman, Harper & Row, 1990

*Vicky Therese Davis, William R. Patterson, D. Marques Patton, The Baron Son, Long & Silverman Publishing, 2005*

*Brian L. Weiss, Ph.D., Many Lives Many Masters, A Fireside Book, Simon & Schuster, 1988*

*Tom Kenyon, Brain States, United States Publlishing, 1994*

*Anthony Robins, Unlimited Power : The New Science Of Personal Achievement*

*Milton H. Erickson, Ed. by Ernest Rossi, The Collected Papers of Milton H. Erickson on Hypnosis, Vol. 1-3, Irvington Publishers, 1984*

*Fred M. Levin, Emotion and the Psychodynamics of the Cerebellum, A Neuro-Analytic Analysis and Synthesis, Karnac, 2009*

*Temple Grandin, C. Johnson, Animals in Translation, Using the Mysteries of Autism to Decode Animal Behavior, Scribner, 1952*

*Ray Kurzweil, Are We Spiritual Machines? Discovery Institute Press, 2002*

*John Searle, The Mystery Of Consciousness, The New York Review Book, 1997*

*John Searle, Consciousness and Language, Cambridge University Press, 2002*

*Mark E. King, Ph.D., Charles M. Citrenbaum, Ph.D., Existential Hypnotherapy, The Guilford Press, 1993*

*Charles Tebbetts, Miracles on Demand, The Radical Short-Term Hypnotherapy, Thomson Shore, Inc., 1995*

Melvin E. Miller, Susanne R. Cook-Greuter, Ed., *Creativity Spirituality and Transcendence, Paths to Integrity and Wisdom in the Mature Self, Alex Publishing Corp, 2000*

Peter Brown, M.D., *The Hypnotic Brain, Hypnotherapy and Social Communication, Yale University Press, 1991*

Mihaly Csikszentmihalyi, *Flow, The Psychology of Optimal Experience, Harper Perenial, Modern Classics Press, 1990*

Jeffrey K. Zeig, PhD, *Experiencing Erickson, An Introduction To The Man and His Work, with Transcripts of Milton H. Erickson, M.D., Brunner/Mazel, 1985*

Jeffrey K. Zeig, Ph.D., Ed. and Comm., *A Teaching Seminar With Milton H. Erickson, Brunner/Mazel, 1980*

Clark L. Hull, PhD., *Hypnosis and Suggestibility, An Experimental Approach, Crown House Publishing, 2002*

David G. Bradley, *A Guide to the World's Religions, Prentice Hall, 1963*

Richard Bandler and John Grinder, *The Structure of Magic, A Book About Language and Therapy, Vol.1-2, Science and Behavior Books, Inc., 1975*

John Grinder and Richard Bandler, *Trance-Formations, Neuro-Linguistic Programming and the Structure of Hypnosis, Real People Press, 1981*

Steve Andreas, Connirae Andreas, *Change Your Mind and Keep The Change, Real People Press, 1987*

Richard Bandler and John Grinder, *Reframing, Neuro-Linguistic Programming and the Transformation of Meaning, Real People Press, 1982*

Richard Bandler, *Using Your Brain For A Change, Real People Press, 1982*

Milton H. Erickson, Ernest L. Rossi, Sheila I. Rossi, *Hypnotic Realities, The Induction of Clinical Hypnosis and Forms of Indirect Suggestion, Irvington Publishers, 1976*

*The Portable Jung*, Edited By Joseph Campbell, *Viking Penguin, 1971*

Gary Klein, *Streetlights and Shadows, Searching for the Keys to Adaptive Decision Making, A bradford Book, MIT Press, 2011*

Nicholas Humphrey, *A history of The Mind, Evolution and The Birth Of Consciousness, Simon & Schuster, 1992*

Dudley Lynch, *The Mother Of All Minds, Leaping Free of an Outdated Human Nature, Brain Technologies Press, 2003*

Elkhonon Goldberg, *The Executive Brain, Frontal Lobes and The Civilized Mind, Foreword By Oliver Sacks, Oxford University Press, 2001*

Gary E. R. Schwartz, Ph.D., Linda G. S. Russek, Ph.D., *The Living Energy Universe, Hampton Roads, 1999*

Candace B. Pert, Ph.D., *Molecules of Emotion, The Science Behind Mind-Body Medicine, A Touchstone Book, Simon & Schuster, 1997*

Jay Haley, *Uncommon Therapy, The Psychiatric Techniques of Milton H. Erickson, M.D., Norton & Co, 1986*

J. Milne Bramwell, *Hypnotism and Treatment by Suggestion, David McKay Publisher, 1889*

John Edward, *Crossing Over, The Stories Behind The Stories, Princess Books, 2001*

*Melvin Morse M.D., Closer To Light, Ivy Books, 1990*

*Raymond Moody, The Light Beyond, Rider Press, 2001*

*Dr. Georgina Cannon, Return, Experience The Power Of The Past, Cannon , 2004*

*Florinda Donner, Being-In-Dreaming, Harper Press, 1981*

*Marie-Lise Labonte, Conversations With Angels, You'll Remember The Love, Blue Pearl Press, 1998*

*Diane Stein, We Are The Angels, Crossing Press, 1997*

*Laeh Maggie Garfield & Jack Grant, Angels and Companions In Spirit, Celestial Arts, 1984*

*Alma Daniel, Timothy Wyllie, Andrew Ramer, Ask Your Angels, A Practical Guide to Working With Messengers of Heaven to Empower And Enrich Your Life, Ballantine Books, 1992*

*Temple Grandin, Animals Make Us Human: Creating the Best life for Animals (with Catherine Johnson, 2009)*

*Frederick Matthias Alexander, The Use Of The Self, Methuen & Co., 1932*

*Moishe Feldenkrais, Awareness Through Movement: Easy-to-Do Health Exercises to Improve Your Posture, Vision, Imagination, and Personal Awareness, Harper Collins, 1972*

*Thomas Hanna, Somatics, De Cappo Life Long Publishing, 1988*

*Paul Ekman, Emotions Revealed, Henry Hold and Company, 2003*

*Michael Gazzaniza, Who's In Charge? Ecco, Harper Collins Publishers, 2011*

*Ande Agassi, Open: An Autobiography, AKA Publishing, 2009*

*Patricia Garfield, Creative Dreaming, 1974*

*Sally Hogshead, Fascinate: The 7 triggers, Harper Collins Publishers, 2010*

# About the Author

Morrin Bass is a founder and director of New York Awareness Center with over a decade of practical experience of working with clients in "gamma" higher consciousness state. Morrin's expertise in hypnotism is sparked by her natural talent and coupled with her extensive training, teaching and client work. Morrin's expert work over a decade allowed her to enjoy success in creating and leading workshops for communities of various backgrounds and beliefs. Her purpose of raising awareness of the role of our authenticity and uniqueness in being ourselves and creating life with purpose.

Born in Moscow, Russia, and received her Ph.D. in architecture, following her parents footsteps and architectural influence. Upon arriving in the U.S. Morrin changed direction and earned her MBA, working for over a decade as a banker and climbing her ladder of success on Wall Street. After a personal crisis in 2001, Morrin had retired from banking and started her own business founding the New York Awareness Center, and opening doors to community as a certified and trained instructor of various alternative modalities.

Morrin is a creative author of a program called Staying in the Light[(tm)], based on her client work over the last decade, and studies of neuro-psychosomatic awareness, integration with daily strategic steps in living with intention. Together with her partner Mark Schwimmer, Morrin enjoys a following of thousands of interested people from all over the world, with whom she works on a private mentoring basis, and teaching in groups, in New York City and traveling around the globe.

Morrin Bass is an international women's provocative and fascinating keynote speaker, lecturer, and workshop leader on subjects of Success and Satisfaction, advocating informed self-awareness, self-empowerment, creativity, and personal responsibility in decision making awareness.

Morrin's life-long interest in oil painting brings her to creating original art inspired by her clients' spiritual visions, which she enjoys making for her exclusive private clientele.